Thomas Ryan

Recollections of an Old Musician

Thomas Ryan

Recollections of an Old Musician

ISBN/EAN: 9783337084417

Printed in Europe, USA, Canada, Australia, Japan

Cover: Foto ©Thomas Meinert / pixelio.de

More available books at **www.hansebooks.com**

THOMAS RYAN.

RECOLLECTIONS OF AN OLD MUSICIAN

BY

THOMAS RYAN

OF THE MENDELSSOHN QUINTETTE CLUB
BOSTON

LONDON
SANDS & COMPANY
1899

DEDICATION

My dear Mr. Brown:

Old friendship alone would warrant me in asking you to stand godfather to this collection of musical memories, yet the appropriateness of dedicating it to you is self-evident, while it gives me great personal satisfaction.

Most of us, or the best of us, may have done fairly well as workers in Boston's musical vineyard, yet it will be found that our labors have produced but ephemeral results in comparison with yours.

Not only have you, for many years, been a participator in forming musical societies, to lay the foundations of a healthy art growth, but a rare foresight impelled you to devote your time, means, and energies to the acquirement of everything relating to music,—its history, its vast literature, and its complete or reduced scores of any value from the earliest compositions to those of to-day. Your collection may fairly be called stupendous; it is a monument to your industry and discrimination.

Having gathered it, you presented this remarkable collection to the citizens of Boston, to form a part of the great stores of learning in the Public Library, and to be forever free to students of music and seekers after musical knowledge. I believe that this act has ennobled you in the eyes of every thoughtful citizen.

As a musician, who foresees the benefits to flow for all future time from your generous and invaluable gift, I beg to assure you of my individual appreciation; and I hope to remain, as ever,

Your friend and fellow-worker,
Thomas Ryan.

To Allen T. Brown, Esquire,
Boston, Mass.

PREFACE

RETROSPECTION is the inheritance of mature age. We all love to recall the scenes of the past and the companions of our pleasures or sorrows. I often order memory to unroll slowly before my mental vision the panorama of my past life. Upon some of the scenes I look with a strong desire to chain the wheels that move them from view, but with others those wheels cannot turn too quickly.

The first picture I call up stands out clearly defined. I see myself as a boy again, landing on America's shore, with the pleasures of hope shining in my eyes,—for a good fairy has touched the new land with her magic wand, and every object I look upon is strangely beautiful.

The same good fairy leads me up State Street and Court Street in Boston, and, wandering aimlessly and boylike, I follow up the hill into Pemberton Square. I stand there and look round at the solid, comfortable, stately mansions of old Boston's aristocracy, and possibly I feel my own insignificance. I get my first glimpse of American female beauty, for, looking into one of the long windows which reach to the parlor floor, I see a charming girl rocking back and forth in a kind of chair which is totally new to my young eyes. I am fascinated, fairly entranced, and doubtless gaping wonder is expressed in my countenance.

It is just fifty years since that trivial event happened, and yet—so wondrously are we made!—in the twinkling of an eye memory gives back the picture perfect in every detail— and just as rapidly will change it for another.

In moments of quiet abstraction I thus call up and dwell on every past event from boyhood to the present. I begin perhaps with sailing on the ship, my landing, my first theatre employment; I pass on to the formation of the Quintette Club and its first concert in Boston, the Jenny Lind visit, the various orchestral experiences, the opening of the Boston Music Hall, our club's first trips out of New England and to the West, my first sight of great Chicago, romantic California, Honolulu, New Zealand and the other Australian colonies, the return to glorious America, the year with Madame Nilsson—and so on and on till all seems on a dead level of monotony; and yet it has been as eventful as most men's lives are when devoid of the heroic or the tragic.

This conjuring up of life's past events before the mind's eye is familiar to all thoughtful persons, but it is a half-dreaming habit and entertains the dreamer only. I hope that it will not be thought that I have rashly undertaken the task of making my dreamy recollections interesting to other people; I think there must be many who would like to know how we of the earlier musical force worked, and what kind of an environment we had fifty years ago. If I succeed in interesting my readers in my recollections, I shall be amply repaid for the labor of jotting them down.

T. R.

BOSTON, March, 1899.

CONTENTS

Chapter I

Boyhood — Musical Training — Violin Episode — Sailing for America — Friends Aboard — Arrival — First Impressions of Boston — Theatre Engagement 1

Chapter II

The American Atmosphere — The Adelphi — John Brougham — The Howard Theatre — The *Matrimonial Galop* — Stock Companies — Mr. and Mrs. Seguin — Musical Education . 11

Chapter III

Father Streeter's Church and Stories — Junius Brutus Booth — A Stage Combat — Incidents of the Stage — The Viennoise Children 20

Chapter IV

Henry Herz, Pianist — Sivori at Home — Paganini's Violin — The Havana Opera Troupe — Arditi and his Admirer — Marti, Pirate, Fish Dealer, and Opera Manager . . 31

Chapter V

The Boston Academy of Music — Its Aims — Rehearsal of *Midsummer Night's Dream* Overture — The Germania Association — Programme of its First Concert in Boston . . 43

Contents

CHAPTER VI

Local Societies—The Musical Fund—The Melodeon—"Old Tom Comer"—His Financial Appeal—Haydn's "Farewell Symphony" 49

CHAPTER VII

Steyermark Orchestra—Francis Riha—Lombardi Orchestra—Saxonia Orchestra—Germania Musical Association—William Schultze—Carl Bergman and his *Up Broadway*—First Public Rehearsals—Typical Programme . . 56

CHAPTER VIII

Influx of Musicians—Gungl Orchestra—Jullien the Conductor—His Versatility—His Character and History—His Performance of *Night* in Crystal Palace, New York . . 65

CHAPTER IX

The Handel and Haydn Society—Mr. John L. Hatton—Mr. Charles C. Perkins—Carl Zerrahn—Dr. J. C. Upham—The "War Secretaries"—B. J. Lang—Margaret Ruthven Lang 76

CHAPTER X

Ole Bull—*The Arkansas Traveller*—Julius Eichberg—The Boston Conservatory of Music 88

CHAPTER XI

Mendelssohn Quintette Club—First Public Concert—Lyceum Lectures and Professor Agassiz—Yankee Singing-Schools and Musical Conventions—Home-bred Talent . . . 92

Contents

Chapter XII

Annie Louise Cary—The Orchestral Union—The Harvard Musical Association—The Boston Symphony Orchestra—Mr. John Bigelow—Mendelssohn Quintette Club Members 101

Chapter XIII

Mr. Jonas Chickering—The White Linen Apron—Upright, Square, Grand Man—Thomas Power—Rufus Choate's Chirography—Invitation Concert 108

Chapter XIV

Lowell Mason—Oliver Ditson—An Accident—John Sebastian Dwight—Dwight's *Journal of Music*—Musical Conservatism 115

Chapter XV

Mendelssohn Birthday Festival in 1851—Newspaper Notices—Youthful Enthusiasm—Beethoven Centenary Commemoration 123

Chapter XVI

Jenny Lind—Her History—How a Poor Boy Earned his Ticket—An Advertising Dodge—Jules Benedict—Belletti—Otto Goldschmidt—Daniel Webster's Bow—Concert in Fitchburg Depot—Jenny Lind at Northampton . . . 128

Chapter XVII

Catherine Hays—Madame Sontag—Carl Eckert—Paul Jullien, the Boy Violinist—Alboni—Hector Berlioz . . 144

Contents

Chapter XVIII

William Lloyd Garrison—Mrs. Garrison—Theodore Parker—Thomas Starr King—Collaboration with Oliver Wendell Holmes—National Hymns 148

Chapter XIX

Changes of the Quintette Club—William Schultze—S. Jacobsohn—Playing for a Sick Man—Schubert's *Swan Song*—"Death and the Maiden" 155

Chapter XX

Trips to Philadelphia, Baltimore, Washington—The Washington Editor—A Musical Criticism—Going West—Elliot's Advertising Feat—A Partnership Poster 162

Chapter XXI

The National College of Music—The Boston Fire—The Lady Lecturer—Travelling Tales—The Young Men's Society—Statuettes Metamorphosed 172

Chapter XXII

The Peace Jubilees—Patrick Sarsfield Gilmore—The Province House—Parepa-Rosa—Drilling Choristers in New England—The "Anvil Chorus"—Programme of First Jubilee Concert 185

Chapter XXIII

The Second Jubilee—Foreign Bands—Political Antagonisms and Musical Rivalry—Madame Pescha Leutner—Madame Rudersdorf—Johann Strauss 198

Contents

Chapter XXIV

Wieniawski—His Style of Playing—Rubinstein—A Musical Evening—A Visit to the Kitchen 204

Chapter XXV

Trip to California—From Snowdrifts to Roses—To Australia—Concert at Sydney, New South Wales—Brisbane, Queensland—Natives and their Characteristics—Maryborough and Gympie—A Smoking Audience . . . 210

Chapter XXVI

Tasmania—Hobart, the Capital—Ascent of Mount Wellington—Launceston—A Paganini Souvenir—Volunteer Settlers, 220

Chapter XXVII

Return to Sydney—An Unexpected Encounter—A Sad Story—Farewell Concert—To Melbourne—Julius Siede—To Adelaide, South Australia—Wellington, Capital of New Zealand—Dr. Hector and the Mountain Lake—The Maoris—Concert at Honolulu—Teresa Carreño . . 227

Chapter XXVIII

Christine Nilsson—Her Genial Character—A Christmas Eve Surprise—Otto Hegner, Boy Pianist 242

Chapter XXIX

Incidents and Happenings—Indian Auditors—Bird Imitation—Noisy Exit at Topeka—Hardships of Travel—The Prairie Schooner—Sleighing under Difficulties—Printers' Pranks 247

Chapter XXX

Some New England Musicians—J. C. D. Parker—J. K. Paine —Ernst Perabo—Arthur Foote—George Sumner . . 259

Chapter XXXI

Soldiers' Home at Milwaukee—Saluting the Stars and Stripes —A Later Visit—"Bully for the Dutch" . . . 266

Chapter XXXII

Joachim the Violinist—*Matinée bei Joachim*—Berlin High School of Music—Playing of Pupils—Americans—L'Envoi, 271

LIST OF ILLUSTRATIONS

	PAGE
THOMAS RYAN	*Frontispiece*
THE RYAN HOME	1
JOHN BROUGHAM AND McCULLOUGH	12
CHARLOTTE CUSHMAN	20
AUGUSTE FRIES	26
SIVORI	32
ALLEN T. BROWN	38
GEORGE JAMES WEBB	46
WILLIAM SCHULTZE	58
MARIE BARNA	66
FRITZ GIESE	72
CARL ZERRAHN	80
B. J. LANG	84
OLE BULL	90
MENDELSSOHN QUINTETTE CLUB, 1849	94
ANNIE LOUISE CARY	101
JOHN BIGELOW	104
JONAS CHICKERING	110
LOWELL MASON	112
OLIVER DITSON	116

List of Illustrations

	PAGE
JOHN S. DWIGHT	120
FELIX BARTHOLDY MENDELSSOHN	126
ANTON HEKKING	132
WULF FRIES	136
JENNY LIND	140
WILLIAM LLOYD GARRISON	148
MRS. GARRISON	152
RUDOLPH HENNIG	158
CAMILLE URSO	164
D. H. ELLIOT	170
MARGARET RUTHVEN LANG	178
PATRICK S. GILMORE	186
PAREPA-ROSA	192
JOHANN STRAUSS	200
HENRI WIENIAWSKI	204
ANTON RUBINSTEIN	206
THE CLUB THAT WENT TO AUSTRALIA, 1881,	212
HOBART, TASMANIA	220
FERN TREES NEAR INVERCARGILL	233
ADELAIDE, SOUTH AUSTRALIA	233
DUNEDIN, NEW ZEALAND	234
LILA JUEL	238
CHRISTINE NILSSON	242
OTTO HEGNER AND HIS FATHER	248
GEORGE W. SUMNER	262
THE MENDELSSOHN QUINTETTE CLUB	266

THE RYAN HOME, HARRISON SQUARE, DORCHESTER.

RECOLLECTIONS OF AN OLD MUSICIAN

CHAPTER I

THE old musician who presents these recollections to the reader believes that there are a goodly number of old-time friends, those who lived in the "fifties," who will share his pleasure in recalling local history of musical and theatrical life.

As a participator in most of the occurrences here detailed, I claim the privilege of writing in the first person, and of introducing myself by a few pages of autobiography. I hope to be credited with modesty; and I will inflict only a small section of my personal history on the reader. I would not do even that were it not that I can fairly be considered a type of the average professional musician. Moved by the same feeling that makes us watch the growth of a tender young plant with interest, we follow with no less interest the growth of the human plant, we try to find out its origin and what has been its environment; knowing that, we make deductions which become part of our stock of knowledge.

One fact is quickly recognized; namely, that the musician who, with enthusiasm and love for the art, works his way to the front, generally comes from the class in which poverty and struggle are born twins, and are ever wrestling with each other; and the persistent wrestler is the one who inevitably overcomes his twin brother, and leaves him behind in the ranks of the lazy and the slothful.

My father was a soldier in the English army. He was a passionate lover of music and played the flute respectably. I naturally infer that I inherited from him my musical temperament. I began to study the flute when I was about nine years old. My father did not own a beginner's book for the instrument, and a friend loaned me one. On a certain Christmas morning I was given a sixpence. With that Fortunatus-gift I trudged three miles from our fort into the town of Kinsale, Ireland, and bought twelve sheets of music-paper, on which I copied the entire instruction book, exercises and all, from cover to cover. It is a trifling bit of history, but shows me conclusively that I was made of the right stuff. I think it is not often recorded that a boy of nine spends his Christmas-gift money to purchase paper in order to copy an instruction book.

What would I not give now to possess that copy! None of us as boys realize how highly we shall prize certain things which were fashioned by our own hands when we were little fellows. We do not foresee the time when some of these trifles will be counted among our dearest treasures.

Until I was ten years old I practically had heard no music, for my father's regiment was away on foreign service with its band. A little later, to my great delight, a regiment with a complete band came to our post. I was on the watch for their first rehearsal; I begged father to take me to it. He and I entered the room just as the band was beginning to play the overture to *Fra Diavolo*. The drum solo with which it begins transfixed me, but when the trumpet solo at the opening *allegro* began, I screamed with delight and father had to put his hand over my mouth to keep me from disturbing the musicians. It is safe to say that a certain little boy was present every time that band played.

When I was fourteen years old, father's regiment returned to England. The band was good, thanks to its skilful master. From that time on I had fairly good and regular training in music. I was placed under the band-master's care, who became a kind of second father to me, and helped me in my ambitious desire to study all the band instruments, but kept me mainly on the clarinet. When I was sixteen years old, I was made to feel very proud by being invited to play second clarinet in the Anacreontic Society of Belfast, Ireland. This was my first playing with anything like a symphony orchestra. The immediate result was to inspire me with an unconquerable desire to study the violin. An incident in connection therewith is perhaps worth recording.

Strolling one day in Belfast, I saw in a pawn-shop window an old violin with a handsome carved head, and, boylike, I desired to own it. I stepped into the shop and inquired the price. It was one guinea. I had in my pocket just ten shillings, which I handed over to the shopkeeper, who gave me a written guaranty that he would hold the violin till I paid him the balance of the money. I went at once to my music-master, told him I needed eleven shillings to buy something not to be mentioned, got the money, bought the violin, carried it to my teacher, and told him I wanted to learn to play the instrument. He was very much pleased, examined the instrument, said it was not of much value, but if I really wanted to study the violin I could use his. This was a valuable instrument that had been in the family for two generations. He paid me back my ten shillings, fitted me out with violin, bow, and the unfailing *Kreutzer Method*, and gave me lessons for about eighteen months, till the regiment was ordered to leave England again for foreign service. We then had to part company. I returned the violin, said good-bye to my dear friend and music-teacher, made a short farewell visit to my family, went to Liverpool, and took passage in a sailing-ship for Boston.

Before going farther with my history, I must say a little more about that violin. About thirty years ago our Quintette Club was engaged for a concert in Montreal. In the concert room some members of my family, who were travelling with us, noticed in the audience an old gentleman of very dignified appearance, who seemed entirely engrossed with the music; when it was my turn to come forward and play a clarinet solo he almost rose to his feet; and while I was playing his handkerchief was in constant use, for tears were running down his cheeks. As soon as the last note of my piece was sounded, the gentleman jumped up, rushed towards the stage, met me face to face, and throwing his arms about me just as I recognized him, he exclaimed, " Tom, my boy!"—and I beheld once more my dear old friend and music master. He had recently been stationed in Montreal, and seeing my name in the announcement of the concert, had been to the hotel to find me; but as our party was late in arriving, he had to wait until the evening before he could see me.

After the concert I went home with him, for we had a thousand things to say to each other. On entering the parlor, there on a centre table lay the old violin with the carved head that I had bought in the pawn-shop in Belfast, Ireland. I examined it, and saw that it was worth very little from a money point of view, but it possessed for me an inestimable sentimental value. I said to my old friend, " I must have that violin."

" No, Tom, you cannot," he answered; "for in all my wanderings since you parted from me, it has generally been the first thing I unpacked. I will tell you, though, what you can have; I will give you the old family violin, the one on which you began to study."

Naturally, I was very much affected by so generous an act. In vain I offered to pay him for the instrument; he would not listen. We passed a couple of delightful hours in relating our happenings; and I had the pleasure of seeing my old friend many times thereafter ere he passed away to join the good people in Paradise.

I have the violin now, and must relate another event in its history. At one period it needed some repairs, and I gave it into the hands of the well-known Mr. Warren White, who had a store and repair-shop in the Tremont Temple. When the instrument was repaired I had it well packed in paper, and a tag with my name attached to it. I then handed it to the storekeeper with the request that he would put it in a safe place while I did some errands. I saw him push it into a sort of pigeon-hole under the front shop-window; then the transaction passed from my mind. Some months later, needing the violin, I opened the case, and was horrified to find it empty. Every member of my family could recall the fact of my taking the violin away to be repaired, but knew nothing further. I remembered getting it from Mr. White, and that was all. I came to the conclusion that I had left it somewhere while attending to my errands, and mourned sincerely the loss of the instrument.

Nearly a year from that time I received notice from Mr. White that he was moving to another store, and that a violin tagged with my name had been found in one of the pigeonholes under his store window. I went with great glee, re-found my old friend, and carried it home in triumph.

To return to my personal history: While on the voyage to Boston, there was very little to interest me outside of my own thoughts. The passengers on a sailing-vessel in those days were not very congenial, and I,—a rather shy boy of seventeen,—though full of curiosity about the new home before me, and of enthusiasm for the profession which was to be my life-work, felt a depressing sense of isolation.

A six weeks' voyage, however, usually brings people together who otherwise would never know or care for each other. It happened that my practice on the clarinet in my stateroom was overheard by some Western people, who became interested, and soon began to like to talk with me. Their kind words quite won my heart, for the homesick " all-alone-in-the world" feeling had taken possession of me, and I was in the mood to welcome friendly advances. These good people tried to induce me to go West, but I had determined to make Boston my home, and would not abandon the idea. Yet often my heart reached out to these friends, and in after years when I met them again and again I found them always staunch and true.

I think I shall never forget my first sight of the city which has been my home for so many years,—it was rapture. Early morning was just dawning when we made Boston Light. The rising sun was shedding its rosy beams on the dome of the State House. The splendid bay and harbor, the picturesque, pleasant homes on the shores, seemed so beautiful in the clear early summer atmosphere that it was just like fairyland to me—the sanguine boy of seventeen and a half years old, who was so soon to try a new life. I was full of faith that everything and every face was to smile on me—and all did smile on me, for even when separating from my ship friends, who were perhaps the first Americans I had ever met, I had their parting benedictions to go with and sustain me for the first few days spent in seeking an engagement.

On the third day from landing, in May,

1845, I was duly engaged as flautist at the Washington Street Theatre, at the very respectable salary of seven dollars per week. Mr. William B. English was the manager. The theatre was on the corner of Winter and Washington streets, over Lee's saloon, now Tuttle's shoe store.

CHAPTER II

THERE was, and is to-day, an indescribable something in the atmosphere of America which gives to the stranger the impression that every one is happy, prosperous, and having a good picnic-like time; while in Europe a more serious and depressing atmosphere exists. I remember distinctly how jubilant the new life and new country made me, and how happy I was to earn so much money and amuse myself evenings by playing in a pretty theatre. The idea of its being labor did not occur to me.

The only souvenirs that I have of that first summer are the little comedies brought out by Mr. English, and his melodrama of *Rosina Meadows*, which first saw light in that little theatre, and had a great run for several years. The two Chapman brothers were very clever, funny people, and were inimitable in the celebrated *Mrs. Caudle's Curtain Lectures*, written by Douglas Jerrold for *Punch* (to which he was a principal contributor), and prepared for the stage by some witty playwright. We had also the well-known Mrs. Drake and her daughter,—the latter a beautiful girl and a wonderful soubrette, who afterward married Harry Chapman. "Gentleman Fenno" was the leading man.

The indulgent reader will permit me to relate here an experience I passed through last winter, while the opera was at the Boston Theatre, which affected me strongly. I was strolling in the corridor between the acts, my eyes idly scanning the old play-bills which hang on the walls, when—lo and behold!—there hangs a play-bill of the little Washington Street Theatre, a programme of a night in July, 1845. I stand transfixed. All the old names and pieces recall the scene to memory so vividly that I am again the youth of seventeen years, breathing the romantic atmosphere in which I then lived. It positively unfitted me for enjoying the rest of the evening. Henceforward I know there is a spot in the corridor which has a special attraction for me.

In the autumn of 1845 Mr. English moved his dramatic company to a small theatre on Court Street, the stage end of which looked into Cornhill, and the auditorium reached to Brattle Street,—all on the second story of the building. The dramatic company comprised many people of genius in their special-

JOHN BROUGHAM AND McCULLOUGH.

ties, including the inimitable John Brougham and his wife; Chanfrau, who was even then famous in his *rôle* of "Mose, the Volunteer Fireman"; Mr. and Mrs. Bland, the two Chapmans, Chippendale, and Miss Drake. The theatre was called the Adelphi. Its main line of work was musical extravaganza. John Brougham tried most of his pieces in Boston long before he moved to New York—pieces like *Pocahontas* and *Cherry and Fair Star*. He composed parodies—even on great works like *Macbeth*,—of which there seemed to be no end. Everything produced was for fun, and Brougham was quite the life and soul of it all. He was to me a wonderful man—handsome, good-natured, and ready-witted.

One night in the course of a piece, he had to hide himself in a large old standard clock and at a given moment rush out in defence of the inevitable young lady in difficulties. Making an incautious rush, he knocked over the old clock and sprawled out on the floor. The hands of the clock flew near to the feet of the stage villain. Brougham, whose ready wit never halted, shouted out, "Even the clock says, 'Hands off!'" You may imagine the roar of laughter which this impromptu sally drew from the audience.

Mrs. Brougham was a handsome, though large and over-fleshy woman. According to stage history, in her younger days she had been an accomplished dancer; and even now she could dance with the aërial agility of a Taglioni. She was also a fairly good singer. All the others were skilled artists, who had been through the training-school of stock companies. They had one and all been selected by Brougham, and were a set of people whose counterparts could not be found in this age.

I played in this little theatre two seasons. Then came promotion. I was engaged to play in the Howard Atheneum, at the munificent salary of nine dollars per week. That theatre had just been built on the site of the "Second Advent Tabernacle." It was said that the builders of the theatre put in the big church window in front, in readiness to convert the building to church uses in the event of its not being successful as a theatre. The "Tabernacle" was a large wooden barn of a building and had for a few years been used for theatre and opera, after the religious delusion had exploded. One very lucky night it burnt down, and then was built the fairly solid Howard Atheneum.

Playing in this new theatre was for me an

agreeable change. It had, for those days, quite a sizable orchestra. The leader sat facing the stage, and was for a long time the only first violin. We had but one second violin, one viola, one contrabass, no violoncello, one flute, two clarinets, one fagott, two horns, a trumpet, a trombone, and drums. The kind and quality of music played would nowadays strike one as queer. It consisted of overtures, quadrilles, polkas, galops—in short, mostly dance music. There was a total absence of so-called popular music, if we except a few quicksteps and marches. There were no characteristic pieces such as figure on the programmes of to-day.

I well remember the first one we were asked to play. It was called the *Matrimonial Galop*. It was of ordinary construction, the only reason for its peculiar name being a sudden hold-up, where the drummer or leader, I forget which, blew into a little instrument that gave out a sound like the cry of a baby. That childish noise made the audience roar with delight, and we had to play it nightly. We poor musicians suffered; but one night we had our revenge. The usual calls came from the audience—they wanted the baby-cry, but did not get it. The machine crying-baby had vanished—

it could not be found. Consternation reigned among those who wanted the people pleased, no matter how it was done. We tried to appease the audience by playing the galop; but when we came to the spot of spots, and there was no realistic baby-cry, but only a base imitation made on the fiddle, a howl of derision and rage went up, equal to anything ever heard in a menagerie. The disappointment was more than the audience could stand.

It was a time in the history of our people when *concessionnaires* were allowed to peddle apples, oranges, candy, and the like, in the upper tiers. The indignant gods of the gallery began to pelt us with their apples and oranges, and we had to leave the orchestra in a hurry. The manager came before the curtain and tried to be funny, but a good half-hour was spent in waiting for quiet. Finally there was a lull in the gale, the curtain rang up, and a piece began. What the manager tried to say to the audience was that some fellow whose baby had died had stolen the machine and carried it home to console the poor dejected mother!

The Howard, of which Mr. Ayling was the manager, had a large stock company. My young readers are not to infer from the word "stock" that a syndicate of capitalists exploited the finances of the theatre. It means, in contradistinction to the present custom of having entire companies of players travel from town to town, that the theatre had its own regular company, and was visited by individual stars, such as Booth (the elder), Macready, Charlotte Cushman, E. L. Davenport, Cora Mowatt, and occasionally a complete opera company, like the Seguins, which I think was the only opera company then travelling in the United States.

We had also visits from ballet companies, at that time very much in vogue. It would doubtless be a strange entertainment for the present age. Imagine people being now asked to spend two or three hours witnessing a play in "dumb show"; though good pantomimic action, artistic dancing, fine scenery, and the best of instrumental music were given. Apropos, I may be allowed to state that the best composers of the period—mostly French —wrote good ballets; notably *Les Wilis*, by Adolphe Adam, composer of *Le Postillon de Longjumeau, Le Châlet,* and many other operas.

Visits from the Seguin Opera Company were a delight to me. The performances were up to a very creditable standard, the singing being in English of course. The list included most of the operas by Balfe, Wallace, Donizetti, Bellini, Auber, Adam, and Boieldieu; such as *Masaniello, Fra Diavolo, Crown Diamonds, La Bayadere, La Sonnambula, The Stranger, Norma, The Pirate, I Puritani, Lucrezia, Lucia, The Daughter of the Regiment,* and *La Dame Blanche.* The only operas with a comic admixture were *The Barber* and the *Elixir of Love.* The educated musician will recognize all these as almost classic works, and our present race of opera singers may well take off their hats in acknowledgment of the ability of their predecessors.

Mrs. Seguin, the leading soprano, was a genuine musician, a worthy sample of the good all-round artist that comes only from England. That means one who was put at the piano in early life, is at home in all piano music, and has studied enough to be a capable harmonist. The next step was voice building,—*solfeggio* in every shape, individual parts in opera and the invaluable oratorio,—each being carried on without undue haste. Such a person matures with a real respect for music as an art. Mrs. Seguin was a comely woman of fresh rosy English complexion, full of grace and vivacity in all her movements, a painstaking actress, industrious in every detail necessary to complete stage preparation, and the life and soul of the company. I cannot recall a better singer, actress, and musician combined in one person. Certainly among our young American singers, in whose training everything which tends to make a thorough musician is generally omitted, not one can be singled out to compare with Madame Seguin in her prime.

Mr. Seguin was also a capital singer and a remarkably good actor. I think that his "Devilshoof" in *The Bohemian Girl* has never been excelled. He had a grand, flexible bass voice, together with a fund of humor that made his *rôles* in *The Barber* and *Elixir of Love* stand out as masterpieces. It is to be understood that opera bouffe, or the so-called comic opera of the present time, was not in existence. Musicians may congratulate themselves thereon, for thus they escaped the "topical song" infliction and other musical rot of this day.

CHAPTER III

I MUST not omit one historic fact, namely, —theatres in Boston were not allowed to give dramatic or operatic performances on Saturdays (too near Sunday!), and that gave us musicians our freedom; hence the custom of devoting Saturdays to society concerts. I recall another fact: several churches did not have organs, so they called in the assistance of the "devil's instruments"—fiddles and cornets—to help the singers. I played the clarinet for two years in Father Streeter's church on Hanover Street. We had a little orchestra composed of a violin (Mr. William Warren), clarinet (T. Ryan), contrabass (Mr. Burdett), and ophicleide (Mr. Cutting).

Old Father Streeter was a good story-teller. One day he told us that he noticed one of his congregation leaning back in his pew and sleeping with his mouth open. A sailor in the gallery discovered the sleeper and his trap-door of a mouth; took a plug of tobacco out of his own mouth, poised it, took aim, and let

CHARLOTTE CUSHMAN.

it drop. It fell into the trap and choked the sleeper, who jumped to his feet in sudden wakefulness. Another time Father Streeter noticed a man with a fiery red head fast asleep, and a small boy directly behind him went through the motions of a blacksmith heating an iron ; he held the imaginary iron close to the red hair, carefully turned it, and hammered it on his knee. Good Father Streeter with much difficulty maintained his gravity.

The managers of theatres, backed up by our worthiest citizens, petitioned the legislature many times to permit matinées on Saturday afternoons. It was finally granted. That entering wedge soon opened the way for the evening performance,—I think in about 1850.

I came near being killed one night in the Howard. The elder Booth was playing the title *rôle* of *Richard the Third*, and was in one of his magnificent moods, when, during the development of a tragedy, he would become so impassioned and exalted that he believed himself to be a real personage in a living drama. At such times there was positive danger for any one on or near the stage. The "Richmonds" had to be good masters of the sword. Booth was of medium size, compact figure, strong, and full of nervous force. He had been known, in some of his stage fights, to chase his antagonist off the stage, around the wings, and onto the stage again; and it required the utmost circumspection on the part of his opponent to avoid being killed.

On the night in question I was in my usual place in the orchestra, helping to play the battle music, with one eye on the stage watching the progress of the combat, which was terribly real. In a wild paroxysm Booth knocked the sword out of Richmond's hand with terrific force; it flew towards the orchestra, grazed the side of my head, and then stuck quivering with its point well embedded in the wooden music-desk directly behind me. I never again sat in the orchestra when any such sword-fight was in progress.

The combat between Richard and Richmond reminds me of a very funny termination to this same scene as I once saw it enacted in a theatre in Toronto, Ontario. Doubtless there are those in that city who will remember the incident, for it happened not many years ago. Richard had the traditional hunch on his royal back, but it had been incautiously made up. During the progress of the famous combat, it was seen to change position, in fact it began to move down to Richard's middle; then came an awful catastrophe,—the hunch fell on the stage! Every one could see that it was made up of an old pair of flannel drawers—tapes and all. When it fell, it spread out in as comical a shape as could have been made of deliberate design. Instantly there was a roar of laughter, enough to almost "raise the roof." The actors tried to go on, but a sudden remembrance of the old drawers would every now and then convulse the audience and make any serious attention to the play impossible. It was a relief when Richard was killed and the curtain rung down.

Naturally many funny things happen in theatres. When I was a boy playing in Alexander's Theatre in Glasgow, Scotland, a piece was on in which a robber figured prominently. A reward had been offered for his head—a well-known ancient custom. He had been caught, duly decapitated, and the head-money paid. At the rising of the curtain for the third act, the ghastly, dead head could be seen on the magistrate's table. In order to have the scene very realistic, the actor who had been the robber was hid under the table, which had a valance reaching to the floor, and through a hole cut in the table-top the robber's head could come up and lie as naturally on it as any dead head. The piece had had a rather long run and the gallery gods were tired of it. The table with the head was placed near the front of the stage. The aforesaid gallery gods —creatures without a conscience—procured some very old, strong Scotch snuff, and through a little blow-pipe they easily blew the snuff down towards the head. Oh, it was a cruel sight to see that poor dead head, with the eyes closed, sneeze and sneeze and sneeze! Actually in the lifting of the head in the sneezing act, we could hear the poor fellow's chin thump the table on the down-stroke. That ended the robber piece.

In the old National Theatre in Boston I saw a similar trick used to kill a piece. The nautical drama of *Black-eyed Susan* was having a rather protracted run. "Sailor Jones," as he was called, was the great artist of his day. Forty or fifty years ago sea-pieces formed a considerable proportion of the melodramas in vogue. *Black-eyed Susan*—written by Douglas Jerrold, well known by all lovers of the nautical drama—has towards the close of the piece a very affecting scene which generally causes sympathetic persons to shed tears. In old times, people were not so *blasé* as they are to-day; it was not an infrequent thing to hear some tender soul sob right out. That would "start all pumps," to use a phrase then in use. The boys in the pit had got tired of "Susan." In the scene when tears began to flow they put up umbrellas in all directions. That caused "Susan" and "sweet William" to retire.

It may be interesting to young people to know that the pit (following the English custom) was where the present parquet is. It was level and slightly lower than the present floor. It was a cheap part of the house, mostly occupied by men and boys. The first circle brought the highest price; the next was like our family circle. The "third row" had rather a bad character. There was a bar attached to this row, where liquors were sold. There was also a bar for the better class somewhere downstairs. It took a deal of fighting to get rid of the bars and the "third row."

Before ending my theatre recollections I must devote a few pages to the Viennoise Children and their visit to Boston in 1847. The troupe consisted of forty-eight children, all girls, whose ages ran from twelve years to about eighteen. These girls were collected in the city of Vienna by Madam Josephine Weiss, an old ballet mistress of one of the theatres.

The children were said to be poor waifs of the Austrian capital, taken up, given a home, educated, and provided for by the old lady. From the large mass of children in her care she selected the shapeliest and prettiest and taught them to dance and to do everything in the choreographic art. The troupe had given some public exhibitions in Vienna, which won the admiration of the connoisseurs, and was now to be turned to good financial account. Some agency brought them to Boston in a sailing-ship—fifty to sixty days' voyage from Trieste. Think of the task of caring for these forty-eight children fifty days and nights on a sailing-ship! They arrived safely in Boston, and were boarded and lodged over "old Peter Brigham's" saloon on Tremont Row, the second house south of Hanover Street.

I used often to see the children, marshalled by the old, stout ballet mistress, who, leaning on a big stick, would give the word "Vorwarts!" and then they would march, two and two, like seminary girls going out for a walk, over to the Howard Atheneum, where they spent the morning studying the art of dancing. It was of course their special line, and the means by which they earned their daily bread.

When rehearsing their pieces in the theatre,

AUGUSTE FRIES.

the old lady usually sat in a chair on the stage near the orchestra leader with her big stick, which was at once her baton of office and her wherewithal to pound the stage while beating time. She was wonderfully spry in her movements; sometimes she would rush in among the children as though she could kill them, but I never saw anything worse than a seeming roughness. We must remember old times and European treatment of children; the adage, "Don't spare the rod and spoil the child," was the rule. To the lookers-on, these children were apparently happy and having a good time.

A few days after the arrival of the troupe the momentous night of opening came. Our orchestra had had no rehearsal with the children (but had studied the music); consequently when the curtain was raised we had our first sight of them. I must confess in advance my inability to describe the beauty of their performance. It was simply ideal. The opening dance was the "Pas des Fleurs," music by Max Maretzek,—then an unknown name in America; he came over from Europe a few years later. The dance consisted of *andante* introduction, a set of five waltzes, and a lengthy *finale*. When the curtain rose, the children were seen to be built up, about thirty of them, in the form of a huge bouquet, round which were two garlands or rings of flowers (children) that swung slowly around the middle mass. Then the latter disentangled themselves and spread out on the stage in bunches, and the animated movement began. Every kind of figure was made by groups of children,— swinging stars, chains, threading needles, and dancing round the May-pole, which with its long colored ribbons remained on the centre of the stage. The music was good. Each waltz had its appropriate dancing figures. The *finale* brought all into a wild, whirling, passionate movement, and it seemed to us at times as if the whole thing must go to pieces; but the artistic plan was perfectly carried out. The "pleasures of memory" were never more thoroughly realized by any one than by me at this moment of writing; after a lapse of over fifty years, the picture of the dancing children is before me in its living, pulsating shape.

The whole audience was seemingly in ecstasy with the performance. The happy, bright faces and the gleeful play of the children stirred up the deepest emotions of the spectators. Many people were in tears. I know that the old oboist at my elbow did not play many notes during the early part of the waltz, for tears ran down his face like rain. When the dance finally ended and the curtain fell, the audience was in a kind of emotional insanity, and gave vent to it in wild applause. The scenes were so wonderfully beautiful, and so unlike anything before witnessed by a majority of the audience, that they felt as if they had had a dream or vision of Paradise.

During the stay of the children they performed many lovely fairy ballets in two or three acts, in which the fascinating story was told by pantomimic action and dancing. One of their most remarkable pieces was termed the "Mirror Dance." Imagine a fine, apparently seamless lace curtain let down from the flies to the stage, about on a line with the second entrance, embracing its entire width and height. Around this net was a gilt border or frame which made the whole resemble a mirror, all the more perfectly because the stage behind the lace was in darkness.

The green curtain rises. The play begins. The children who perform represent an equal number of boys and girls. One or two couples shyly stray onto the stage in front, and there are exactly similar figures and movements on the inner side of the lace curtain. The front couples discover themselves reflected in the mirror; they are frightened and jump back—the rear ones of course doing the same. The children on both sides, in shape, dress, and action, are such perfect counterparts that the effect is precisely as if done in front of a real mirror. This little tentative work is repeated a few times, but finding that the reflection does not harm them they fear it no more; they grow bold; they come on in larger numbers; they look in the mirror, admiring themselves and their graceful movements, meanwhile going through with many comical performances. Remembering that everything done before the lace curtain is duplicated behind it, we can see that the effect would be wonderful and beautiful. The thing could only be accomplished where girls in large numbers could be selected, matched, and taught with most patient industry.

I cannot say what became of the company after it left Boston. We had no *Dramatic Mirror* in those days.

CHAPTER IV

IN my early years in Boston, foreign artists, singers, and players, came to the United States pretty much as they come now, but relatively in smaller numbers. Boston was even then quite a Mecca for instrumentalists.

Among those who made the greatest impression on me were three genuine artists who formed a little company,—Sivori, violinist, Knoop, violoncellist, Henry Herz, pianist. The latter was spoken of with great acclaim by the newspapers as the composer of variations on *Home, Sweet Home*. His position was thereby fixed at the top round of the art ladder. He did play his own compositions quite neatly, also those of Rosellen and kindred composers, and I was present when he took part in a piano trio by Haydn; but I fear his playing would not pass muster in these days. The 'cellist, Knoop, was of the regulation pattern of well-trained virtuosi, who could play the elder Romberg's compositions. But Sivori was really a master violinist—an advance Wieniawski, without the latter's ability to compose violin music. Sivori had a marvellous technique. He had been the only pupil and protégé of Paganini, and he played on the latter's famous Stradivarius, left by will to him.

In the summer of '88, I spent a part of the season in Paris. Sivori was still alive, and, like the majority of artists who lead the lives of virtuosi, had made Paris his home. I determined to do myself the honor of calling on him, and had an opportunity to do so in company with a Boston friend who knew him well. Sivori was living on the fourth or fifth story of a very modest hotel, having a single room, with space for an upright piano and an alcove for his bed. It was a charming, cosy little room, just such a one as the majority of bachelor artists occupy in Paris, no matter how ample their income; and in these quarters they receive the visits of princes and people of the *haute noblesse*.

I let my friend, who was intimate with Sivori, do the talking for some time, while I watched all the artist's motions. He was a rather small-sized man, and had very small hands for a violinist, at which I marvelled, for his distinction was based on his being a Paganini player; and we all know that the music of that com-

CAMILLE SIVORI.

poser requires the fingers of a prestidigitator. As we progressed in our call I nudged my friend (according to previous agreement) to tell Sivori I was a member of the Mendelssohn Quintette Club of Boston, and that I wanted very much to see the famous "Strad," the inheritance from Paganini. Sivori was amiability itself.

I should have said at the start that he was preparing to sally forth for his *déjeuner* when we called, but he did not hesitate to receive us, though he was at the moment in the most unconventional of costumes. He was the gentleman and *bon camarade* from first to last.

Sivori took out the violin from its case. It was a perfect "Kohinoor" of an instrument, just the right color, and perfectly preserved,—not a scratch or a crack,—with the great seal of red sealing-wax on the under part of the violin where the neck begins. I told Mr. Sivori that I heard him in his first concert given in the old Masonic Temple in Boston (where R. H. Stearns & Co.'s store now is), that I was an enthusiastic boy at the time, and that his playing had made such an impression on me that I could name the pieces he played in that concert, though there was an interim of about forty years. I named them,—the E-flat concerto (his own composition), *La Campanile* by Paganini, and the *Mosé in Egitto*, also by Paganini.

The old artist opened his bookcase, took out a book containing an itinerary of musical *tournées* made in his younger days, and turned at once to Boston. I had named the pieces exactly, and he was highly pleased. He played for us a great deal, and it was a joy to hear the tone of that violin; it was also impossible not to be affected by the sentiment connected with it. Paganini's violin! the instrument of that strange and wonderful player, the wizard of the concert stage, who had conquered all musical Europe.

My friend and I began to feel that we must not prolong our visit, but Sivori wanted to show us his numerous presents received from kings and courts. He told us some very funny stories, one of which I will repeat.

The famous *impresario*, Ulman, well known in America, had engaged four of the greatest living violinists for a little concert trip. It was arranged that at their concerts these virtuosi should each play a solo and then play together the well-known concerto for four violins by Maurer. One night Sivori was greatly dissatisfied with the trill he had made in the famous *Trill du Diable* by Tartini.

Leonard, an equally famous violinist, and he were sharing a very large room in the hotel. Sivori was nervous and could not sleep. The trill haunted him; he got out of bed, partly dressed himself, took out his fiddle, put a mute on it, and, going to the remotest corner from where Leonard lay peacefully sleeping, he began practising the trill in the softest *pianissimo*. Doubtless he made a peculiar, scratchy, mouse-nibbling kind of noise, and it awoke Leonard, who, thinking it was a mouse, reached out for one of his boots and fired it at the corner in order to scare away the supposed mouse. It was a good shot, for it hit Sivori in the middle of the back, causing an outcry which prevented Leonard from making a second shot. The two comrades had something to laugh over for quite a while.

To return to the fact that I had been able to name the pieces played by Sivori after so long an interim: it may seem extraordinary. It is, and yet is not. I argue that any young lawyer who heard Daniel Webster or Rufus Choate speak for the first time would remember to the end of his days the subject of either's oratory.

In the summer of 1847, we had a visit from

a very complete Italian opera troupe. At that period of Boston's social history, it was not the fashion to leave the city for the summer; therefore the citizens were as eager to welcome a good entertainment in summer as in winter.

This Havana troupe was notable for its corps of fine singers, among them being some of the world's foremost artists. Tedesco, the soprano, was truly a great dramatic singer. After the Boston season was over, she went to Paris, and easily won the first place in all European opera houses. Then there was Vita, the contralto, a splendid singer, second only to Alboni. Then came Perelli, the tenor, who was a fine singer, a thorough musician, and a remarkable pianist. This artist after leaving Boston made his home in Philadelphia. There was also Novelli, a magnificent basso, who became well known in Boston, as he visited that city many times subsequently.

The opera had a good effective chorus, and a complete orchestra, with Arditi (afterward so well known) as *maestro*, or conductor, and first violin,—it being the custom in those days for the leader to beat time with his bow, playing on his violin when he desired to assist or to animate his men. This fashion still prevails in many parts of the world. Johann Strauss, the famous waltz composer, played the violin when conducting his compositions in the second Gilmore Jubilee. His brother Eduard, who more recently visited this country with his own orchestra, conducted in the same way. I must not omit to say that Arditi was a true virtuoso on the violin.

To return to our little history of the Havana Opera Company. They had for contrabasso the world-renowned Bottesini, a veritable Paganini on his big instrument. The troupe performed but three times per week. That also was the prevailing custom of the day.

The company supported itself on those three performances, and yet the prices of admission were only fifty cents and one dollar; the former admitting to the gallery. We can infer that the honorariums to the artist were modest in comparison to those of the present day. It may be added that their social standing was quite different from what it is now. Most of them lived in the Pemberton Hotel, adjoining the theatre, and it was certainly a hotel of modest pretension.

It was customary for the troupe to give concerts in the theatre on Saturday evenings, on which occasions Arditi and Bottesini played solos. On one of those evenings a very droll incident occurred. While Arditi was performing a violin solo on the stage, a gentleman in the balcony nearest the stage became so excited over Arditi's *tours de force* that in order to manifest his approbation he resorted to a most extraordinary device. He began by throwing his white kid gloves at Arditi's feet, then his light walking-cane, and finally his hat. I forget whether his coat and vest did or did not follow; certainly it seems as if that would have been a natural sequence. At this juncture a couple of ushers came upon the scene, and great applause and cheering went up from the audience; but whether for Arditi or his admirer in the balcony I cannot say. For a long time, "Oh, take my hat!" was a popular slang phrase.

About a dozen years ago I called on Mr. Arditi in New York, on his return to America as director with Madame Patti. When my card was handed him he was talking with a number of brother artists. I was politely received, and introduced to the gentlemen; and after a few minutes of conversation with Arditi I asked him if he remembered the scene in the Howard Theatre when the man in the balcony began throwing his outfit on the stage.

ALLEN T. BROWN.

The moment I put the question he recalled the incident with great amusement; and, with a zest and volubility possessed only by Italians, retold the story to the artists present, who greeted it with outbursts of laughter.

Returning again to the Havana Opera Company, there was a story current (remember that humbug is as old as the world and that skilful agents were even then industriously "working up business") that Marti, the manager, had been for many years a terror to the island of Cuba, and indeed to the entire West India Islands, as pirate and smuggler, a veritable buccaneer—a kind of man who really once existed in the flesh; nor is it so very many years ago since gentry of his kind operated in all the southern waters. To the city of Havana Marti was a pest. No vessel could go in or out of the harbor without paying tribute to him. The Governor-General of Cuba offered a large reward for Marti's head, dead or alive. The reward did not bring the head. There was no change for a long time in the pestiferous ways of Marti.

Finally an envoy of his reached the Governor with a message to the effect that Marti was tired of his profession and wished to make the following proposition:

He, Marti, would give up his terrible trade, destroy all other pirates in the vicinity, and become a good citizen of the city of Havana, if they would pardon him in full for all previous misdeeds. By way of proper compensation for the loss of so profitable a business, he hoped the Governor would allow him the monopoly of the fresh-fish trade of the city of Havana. Such a monopoly in a large Catholic community means a great fortune. As a *quid pro quo*, Marti would support, for a term of years, an Italian opera company made up of the finest artists, without any subvention from the government or aristocracy of the island.

The proposition was disdained at first and the piracy was continued. Eventually a compromise was effected; the free opera was too tempting a bait not to be eagerly swallowed by people of the Spanish and Cuban temperament. Marti opened the fish-market, carried out all his promises, and became a law-abiding citizen. In due time he collected a bona fide opera troupe, which delighted the citizens of Havana for years.

Something inspired Marti to bring his troupe to Boston. They came from Cuba in a sailing vessel, and gave opera at the Howard Theatre for about two months during two consecutive summers. The average of the performances was good. The operas were by Verdi, Bellini, Donizetti, Mercadante, Rossini—all up-to-date Italian works. The troupe was well supported, being a great novelty and delight to Bostonians; it was also the advance-guard of the many opera troupes afterward brought to our city by enterprising managers.

Is there not a tempting chance here for some lover of that side of the art to write a brief history of the various opera troupes which have visited this country? They have done their share of inculcating a taste for music.

For a while opera meant Italian music only; then, with *Martha* and *Stradella*, came a sprinkling of the lighter class of German operas. The mixture was healthy and prepared our people for the greater things yet to come. Finally the red-letter day dawned which brought me a degree of happiness that I shall never forget. Max Maretzek had an opera troupe in the Federal Street Theatre. He brought out Mozart's *Don Giovanni*, with the fine singer Bosio as "Zerlina." Perhaps my pleasure was heightened by the fact that the director used my score. The copy is one of the earliest published, with the German title-page, *Don Juan; or, The Stone Ghost; a*

Comic Opera in Two Acts. Some few years later, *Fidelio*, by Beethoven, was performed in the Boston Theatre, and at last we heard the **finest** music-dramas; and probably no greater enjoyment will ever be derived from any future performance of them than we got from that first one. Of that I am satisfied.

CHAPTER V

IN my early days in Boston, series of concerts were given in the Federal Street Theatre, on the corner of Franklin Street, by the so-called Boston Academy of Music. There was always a goodly number of music-lovers in Boston,—and we cannot give too much credit to the pioneers who did the ploughing and seeding of musical taste. "The Boston Academy of Music" was formed and named in 1833, by Messrs. William C. Woodbridge, Lowell Mason, and a few kindred souls, who laid out this ambitious but beneficent programme:

1. To establish schools of vocal music and juvenile classes.

2. To establish similar classes for adults.

3. To form a class for instruction in the methods of teaching music.

4. To form an association of choristers and leading members of choirs for the purpose of improvement in church music.

5. To establish a course of popular lectures on the nature and object of church music.

6. To have scientific lectures.
7. To give exhibition concerts.
8. To introduce vocal music into schools.
9. To publish circulars and essays.

The Academy, after a few years of action on this basis, resolved itself into an organization of music-lovers and amateur instrumentalists, assisted by professionals, making an orchestra of perhaps forty, and gave concerts.

The programmes were of very mixed music, but aspiring to the best. Beethoven's *Fifth Symphony* was brought out by them for the first time in Boston. Each programme was generally made up of a French opera overture, one or two instrumental solos by members of the orchestra or strangers, a movement from an easy symphony, a potpourri, and a few vocal pieces.

The President of the Society, at the time of which I am writing, was Gen. B. F. Edmands, a most amiable man and an efficient worker. I was engaged by him as one of the second violins. He saw that I was an ambitious boy, and took a fancy to me. That ambition got me into a little trouble later on, and was the cause of a bit of musical history of the times worth recording.

Before coming to Boston I had played second clarinet in the Dublin (Ireland) Philharmonic

Society. In the season of 1844–45, that Society brought out the *Scotch Symphony* and the *Midsummer Night's Dream* overture, by Mendelssohn. When I made the acquaintance of General Edmands, I took the liberty of telling him that Mendelssohn's music was in great favor in Europe, and urged him to get the above works. They were sent for. When received, it was discovered that no score had come.

We must remember that fifty years ago there were not many professional musicians of sufficient technical ability to cope with Mendelssohn's music, which even to-day is classified as difficult. Our orchestra was made up half of amateurs and half of professionals. We could have no lightning-express trains in *tempo;* most music was played *tempo commodo*. All trains were accommodation trains. "Music was made for man, and not man for music." Those were the governing principles, and in general furnished the motive power.

One other point to remember is the fact that in old days an overture generally meant a big, noisy, pompous, slam-bang affair, intended for a curtain-raiser to an opera,—a certain festive noise to be made while people were tumbling into their seats, or looking around to see who had come, etc. This type of overture was the only one the average player had any acquaintance with; indeed, in point of history, we must not overlook the fact that Mendelssohn was the creator of the so-called romantic overture, under which head come *Fingal's Cave, Calm Sea, Ruy Blas*, etc. Therefore, when I say that the *Midsummer Night's Dream* was taken up for the first time by our orchestra, all cultured persons who are familiar with that delicate, fairy-like composition may well smile to think that any but experts should attempt the difficult feat of playing it.

Well, we tried it. Our conductor was Mr. Geo. J. Webb,—an excellent general musician, but who had never heard the overture. He began by telling us that he had no score; so he stood up alongside of the first-violin desk and prepared to conduct. Rapping on the desk, he gave the signal to begin; out piped two flutes,—nothing else. He rapped again, implying that the players had not been ready to begin; then he said, "We will try again." He gave the signal—and out piped the two flutes. That caused a little titter of surprise, and we all looked quizzically at each other. Mr. Webb, however, dutifully gave the signal for the next "hold" or chord, when two clarinets joined the two flutes! More surprise. At

GEORGE JAMES WEBB.

the third hold (chord) the fagotti and horns were added, and at the fourth hold (chord) the entire wood and wind instruments, all sounding most distressingly out of tune. This dissonant and unlooked-for result was followed by a dead pause; then every one of the players broke out with a hearty laugh of derision.

I was on pins and needles and muttered, "Go on, go on!" After a while the people sobered down, and we tried to commence with the string part. The first and second violins (each relative part divided into two parts) began at an "accommodation-train" *tempo*. At the end of the violin passage, the wood and wind again held a very dissonant chord for two measures, which this time sounded so abominably out of tune that it really was as bad as if each man played any note he pleased; and it was so irresistibly funny that again everybody burst out laughing. But I buried my head under the music desk and cried; my idol was derided, every one poked fun at me.

That last dissonant chord ended the first rehearsal of the *Midsummer Night's Dream* overture. We never tried it again.

Time, however, set me right. A few years later, the Germania Musical Society visited Boston. The Germania was a fine orchestra of about thirty artists, and every one could play well his part. Their first concert was given on April 14th. Their *pièce de résistance* was the overture to *Midsummer Night's Dream*, and it was beautifully played. So I had my revenge and could poke fun at my fellow-players by saying, "Now you can hear what Mendelssohn is as a composer." (The overture was written in 1826, when he was only seventeen years old, as everybody should know.)

This is the programme of the Germania concert:

1. OVERTURE TO "ZAMPA" . . . *Hérold.*
2. WALTZ, "The Pesther" . . . . *Lanner.*
3. FANTAISIE FOR VIOLIN . . . . *Ernst.*
   MR. WM. SCHULTZE.
4. BETTY POLKA . . . . . . *Lenschow.*
5. OVERTURE, "Midsummer Night's Dream," *Mendelssohn.*
6. VARIATIONS ON SWISS AIR FOR THE FLUTE, *Boehm.*
   MR. PFEIFFER.
7. FINALE, "Siege of Corinth" . . . *Rossini.*
8. FESTIVAL OVERTURE, Dedicated to the President of the United States, General Taylor . *Lenschow.*
9. WALTZ, "Sounds from the Heart" . . *Strauss.*
10. PANORAMA OF BROADWAY, NEW YORK. "A descriptive potpourri, received with the greatest applause by large and fashionable audiences," arranged by . . . . . . *Lenschow.*

CHAPTER VI

I AM well aware that I am not writing quite in chronological order. I never kept notes, and do not know a person who can set me right if I put anything on record awry. I am almost the last of the "old guard." I was for many years the youngest musician in Boston; now perhaps I am the oldest, and still in harness. I can make a fair record, in substance, of the rise and fall of the different societies, and that is about all the value which can be attached to it.

Contemporary with the Academy of Music was the Philharmonic Society. The former was under the guidance of men like Mr. Geo. J. Webb, Mr. Lowell Mason, Mr. Woodbridge, Mr. John S. Dwight, and Gen. B. F. Edmands. The Philharmonic was, I think, a younger society, with Mr. Edward Riddle as President,—a well-known amateur flute-player, father of Mr. Geo. Riddle, the elocutionist. The musical director was Mr. Schmidt,—a good musician and a violin virtuoso. I think that each society had from four to six years of life before it went to pieces.

On the ruins of these two societies was organized and incorporated "The Musical Fund Society" in the year 1852. It was composed exclusively of professionals, and was the first society so organized in Boston. It was chartered by the State of Massachusetts and empowered to hold property to a certain amount and to give concerts in aid of sick members. The chief officers were members of the Society, but there was a board of directors and council of advice chosen from the most active and prominent music supporters, perhaps seventy-five in number.

The Society began its concerts in the old Melodeon Hall, where Keith's Theatre now stands, next door to the Boston Theatre. The finances were managed on the co-operative plan; that is, there was an equal division of the profits, the man at the drums getting just as much as the leader of the violins. The director received no pay, the honor being considered a sufficient reward. Soloists who were members of the Society received an honorarium of fifteen dollars.

The "rise and fall" in the history of all such societies is so monotonously similar that one grows weary of writing about it. The Musical Fund, which was no exception to the rule, started off with flying colors and a large subscription, every one rushing to put their names on the list. The orchestra, which numbered about fifty players, did fairly good work for the times. The symphonies played were by Pleyel, Haydn, and Kalliwoda; also the easy ones of Mozart and the early ones of Beethoven. Every musical person can imagine the kind of music given. The orchestra had the assistance of vocal soloists, both foreign and native.

The first two seasons' concerts were given in the Melodeon. This hall, which held about nine hundred and was admirable for sound, proved to be too small to hold the audiences, so the Society moved to the Tremont Temple, which accommodated about fifteen hundred persons. After a few seasons of popularity there was a falling off in the attendance, followed by two seasons that ended without any money to divide; but we kept on all the same, for we had not formed the Society to make money, but rather to improve ourselves in the art of music. A good many small gifts of money came from patrons, and the munificent sum of a thousand dollars was contributed by Jenny Lind.

The Society gave concerts for about six years, but was plainly *moribund*. The Germania Musical Society, which had been in Boston for two seasons, really gave the *coup de grâce* to the Musical Fund Society by its fine orchestra and its superior performances.

Our Society, having resolved to give no more concerts, was changed into a benefit organization. The money in the treasury was liberally paid out to sick members or for funeral expenses, and in donations to widows; one after another the members dropped out, and when the money was gone, all was over.

Many of my pleasantest memories are connected with the workings of the Fund Society. Mr. Webb was the first conductor, followed by "old Tom Comer." The latter, a character in Boston, was well known and beloved. He was of Irish extraction and originally an actor. He had a passion for music—could compose a little, played the violin tolerably well, was leader of an orchestra in the Boston Museum for many years, and afterwards in the Boston Theatre. He was just the man for the times,—popular on all sides, "hand and glove" with every one, as the old saying went, and was a valuable president for the Fund Society.

One of his financial appeals in behalf of the Society is worth putting on record. He decided to perform Haydn's *Farewell Symphony*. To explain the origin and character of this piece of music I must give a bit of history.

In the " good old days " our grandfathers used to talk about, when kings, princes, and prelates of the European states were leeching the life-blood out of the people, every aristocratic worthy lived on a big, showy scale, surrounded by a large retinue of followers, including musicians. Every grandee had his own orchestra, or its equivalent on a somewhat lesser scale. The most famous composers and musicians of the day were in the service of some prince or nobleman. For them no other life was possible; if they did not have the patronage, or were not under the wing, of the high and mighty, they had no way nor right to live. Mozart served for a while with the Bishop of Salzburg, and Haydn served his long life with Prince Esterhazy. To this unfortunate, or perhaps fortunate system, as we choose to look at it, may be attributed the marvellous amount of chamber music written by those composers. New work for the entertainment of guests must be always forthcoming.

It happened that at one period in the life of

Esterhazy his finances were in a pinched condition, and he had determined to discharge a goodly portion of his orchestra. That struck grief and sorrow into the heart of Haydn, and he determined to write a suitable farewell symphony. He composed it and produced it before the court. The symphony was scored at the beginning for the usual number of players, but in the course of its performance the audience noticed that two bassoons, two oboi, and two clarinets quietly shut up their books, put the extinguishers on their candles, and retired very softly and sadly. Other couples did likewise till only a quartette of the strings remained. Haydn, who had appeared to be absorbed in his work as conductor, suddenly discovered that he was left almost alone, looked round in sorrow, heaved a big sigh, and ended the performance. History relates that the ruse was successful; the scene was so pathetic that the Prince concluded to retain his orchestra.

This pretty little drama was re-enacted by the Fund Society in the old Tremont Temple; but alas! there was no prince to come to the rescue. The Society had evidently served its time and purpose, and shortly after it ceased active operations.

One stroke of misfortune was reserved for

the close of its career. On a Saturday night in the coldest part of the winter, the Society gave a concert. When it was over the musicians discovered that the streets were in a very slippery and dangerous condition from the rain that froze as it fell, and a large number of them, fearing to carry their instruments to their homes, left them in the office of the Temple. That part of the building took fire that very night, and all the instruments, music, and properties of the Society were destroyed.

CHAPTER VII

IN the winter of 1846 the first moderately complete orchestra, known as the Steyermark Orchestra, came to the United States from Europe. They numbered about twenty men, good players, with Francis Riha as first violin and director, who afterward became the second violin of the Mendelssohn Quintette Club. They played mostly light dance music, overtures, potpourris, and solos. They did everything with great "chic" or "snap," which was a new thing to our people.

Riha was an exceedingly handsome young man, graceful in every motion, very talented in composition, and a fine violinist. The artists wore the picturesque Steyermark country uniform. They had little clinking, cymbal-like bits of metal attached to the heels of their long boots, and when playing certain characteristic pieces they used to knock their heels together and produce a clear, lively sound which "took" with the audience. They played nightly for about a month in the old Melodeon and then went off on a concert tour. They returned to Boston after a while, but the novelty was gone, and their concerts were poorly patronized, so they soon bade us farewell and once more started out to "seek their fortunes." One after another the performers finally dropped out of the company and settled in various cities, the director, Francis Riha, coming back to Boston.

Sometime in 1848, another organization, styling itself the Lombardi Orchestra, visited us. It was made up of the remnants of an Italian opera orchestra which had ended operations in New York, and came to Boston on a venture, with August Fries as leader and first violin.

It met its fate in Boston and went to pieces; some of the artists remaining there, chief among whom was Mr. Fries, a valuable musician, who became the main founder and leader of the Mendelssohn Quintette Club.

The next orchestra which came to our city was the Saxonia, with Mr. Carl Eckhardt as leader. They played well, but had no financial success, and disbanded in Boston; many of their best men, such as Messrs. Eichler, Stein, Pinter, and the leader, settled there. Mr. Eckhardt was an excellent musician and violinist. He remained in Boston for a number of years, then moved to Columbus, Ohio, and has been up to date the director of music in that city.

In April, 1848, an orchestra which held together six years came to this country, and became quite famous,—the aforementioned Germania Musical Society. It numbered about thirty artists, Mr. Lenschow being the leader. They played much classic music,—their "crack piece" being the *Midsummer Night's Dream* overture. The orchestra was made up of genuine, fine artists, among them Mr. William Schultze, who became the first violin of the Mendelssohn Quintette on the retirement of August Fries in 1859—the tenth year of the Club.

Schultze was about twenty-two years old when he first came to Boston. He had a good, lithe figure, and a handsome, prepossessing face—a face which easily flushed and showed every feeling of modesty or pleasure. It is easy to infer that female admiration laid siege to the heart of this ideal "first violin," and he became the pet of musical Boston. He was a fine violinist, a good general musician, something of a linguist, always a student, yet a most genial, society-loving person, and one of the best story-tellers in the world.

WILLIAM SCHULTZE.

Schultze was the first violin of the Quintette Club for nearly twenty years.

There were other good men and artists of the Germania who must also be remembered. Carl Zerrahn was first flute,—a fine player and an excellent man in every relation of life. He is too well known all through the country to need any panegyric from me. Carl Bergmann made his first appearance with the Society as trombonist, afterward as 'cellist, and was also a good violinist and pianist. Carl Sentz, the leading second violin, was afterward director of music in Philadelphia for many years.

Mr. Carl Meisel, the "well-beloved" in Boston, played at the same desk with Schultze. He succeeded Mr. Riha as second violin with the Mendelssohn Quintette, 1854, in the fifth year of the Club.

When the Germania Society came to America they played part of a season in New York and Philadelphia, and then came to Boston, where they gave a lengthy series of concerts, extending over an entire season. The following season they went to Baltimore and had a similar success. Mr. Lenschow, the leader, finally resigned and settled there.

Carl Bergmann succeeded Lenschow as conductor. He was a talented composer, and was distinctly a man of great attainments in every line of the art of music. Like Mr. Lenschow, he was a wonderful arranger of musical compositions calculated to win popularity,—an essential thing for all artists who have to work for their bread and butter,—among which was a potpourri called *Up Broadway* that became a great favorite. It was supposed to be a graphic tone-picture of sights and sounds seen and heard from Castle Garden to Union Square, which was at that time the boundary of New York's bustling life.

This potpourri began with a musical picture of Castle Garden, which was the home, and the only one, good music had at that time in that city. Moving up with the musical diorama, you next came to Barnum's Museum, with "Barnum's Band" of six or eight brass instruments, which, as all old New Yorkers know, played all day long on a high balcony outside his Museum on Broadway, nearly opposite the Astor House. It was side-splitting to hear the imitation of this brass band. One can even now occasionally enjoy a faint resemblance of it in passing a dime museum.

The report was current that Barnum's players were made to pay a little money for the privilege of practising and playing in public. I don't vouch for its truthfulness, but the story went that a man made application to play the trombone on the balcony with the combination, who, like all musicians, was a very modest man, and did not like to mention the word pay or salary. He was told that he could play. At the end of the week he plucked up courage enough to appear before Mr. Barnum and timidly ask for his wages. Phineas was quite ready with his little bill *per contra:* "John Smith, to P. T. Barnum, Dr., for the privilege of playing on the balcony of Museum one week in public, nine dollars."

Returning to the potpourri, a firemen's parade with brass band came next. Naturally it was preceded by a violent ringing of firebells, and a rushing down a side street with " the machine." When that noise died away, music from the open door of a dance hall was heard; with of course all its accompaniments, —the rhythm of dancing feet, and the calling out of the figures. Then, moving on with the diorama, we passed by a church whence came the sound of organ music and the chanting of a service by a number of voices. After that we heard in the distance a faint kind of Turkish patrol music; then a big *crescendo* and sudden *fortissimo* introduced us to Union Square and its life; and two brass bands in two different keys prepared our nerves for the usual collision and fight between two opposing fire companies. This latter made a great sensation. Finally, fireworks were touched off, the *Star-Spangled Banner* was played, and the potpourri ended, sending every one home in smiling good-humor.

The Germania was a big success in Boston. Subscription lists twenty feet long (no exaggeration) could be seen in the music stores for a series of twenty-four Saturday evenings, and the same number of public rehearsals on Wednesday afternoons. These public rehearsals were the first ever given in Boston, and, if I mistake not, the first given anywhere. Certainly the system did not prevail in Europe, for I distinctly remember that some combination carried out the idea in London, and it was commented on there as "following the American plan."

The Germania held together about six years —most of the time in Boston. They made many short trips in New England, and one *tournée* with Jenny Lind. Their summers were profitably spent in Newport. In the last two seasons they added as stars the famous girl-violinist, Camille Urso, and Alfred Jaell, pianist. Madame Urso is too well known to need any eulogy at my hands. She is one of the very few young wonders who developed into great artists at maturity. Jaell was a splendid pianist. If he were playing at the present day, he would bear comparison with the greatest living players. When the Germania disbanded, he went to Paris, made his home in that city, and won a popularity which he never lost. He died very recently.

The Germania were the first to play in Boston the *C-Major Symphony* of Schubert, the *Ninth Symphony* by Beethoven, and the *Tannhäuser* overture.

In 1854 the Society disbanded. The men were tired of travelling; they wanted to settle down; and the cities of Baltimore, Philadelphia, New York, and Boston were enriched by their presence. Bergmann went to New York, and was elected conductor of the New York Philharmonic Society, which position he held for many years. He died about twelve years ago.

I give a copy of the programme of a typical concert given by the Germania, January 28, 1854; assisted by Mrs. Emma A. Wentworth, soprano, and Mr. Robert Heller, pianist.

1. Jubel Overture . . . . . *Lindpaintner.*
2. Valse . . . . *Strauss.*
3. Terzetti, from "Attila" . . . *Verdi.*
4. Cavatina . . . . . *Meyerbeer.*
   Mrs. Wentworth.
5. Rondo for Piano . . . . *Mendelssohn.*
   Mr. Heller.
6. Potpourri . . . . . *Bergmann.*
7. Quadrille . . . . . . *French.*
8. Overture, "Midsummer Night's Dream,"
   Mendelssohn.
9. Galop . . . . *Lumbye.*
10. Song, "List to the Lark" . . . *Comer.*
    Mrs. Wentworth.
11. Overture, "Siege of Corinth" . . *Rossini.*

Tickets, 50 cents.   Begin 7.30.

CHAPTER VIII

THE success of the Germania was the cause of much trumpeting all over Europe that America was a country which wanted music and would pay for it. The Revolution of 1848 made a big *bouleversement* of everything social and political. Many people had to leave their country suddenly, and the great wave of emigration from continental Europe then began. Germany, Austria, France, and Italy were in a frightful financial and political condition, brought on by the epidemic of revolution, which was in plainer language an aspiration for freedom. That "gasp" was choked for a while, but the spirit is still "marching on." Many of our best immigrant musicians came to America at that period; among whom were the Germania, and, one year later (in 1849), the famous Gungl Orchestra, from Berlin, with the composer at its head. Their venture was a *fiasco*. The orchestra numbered about twenty-five. They did not play so well as the Germania, consequently did not have the elements of a possible success. About the only souvenir I have of their visit is the hour I spent at the first rehearsal of the new waltz *Traum des Oceans*—a fine waltz, probably Gungl's best, which was written while on his voyage to America. Gungl did not give many concerts in Boston, and I think that shortly after his visit he returned to Germany. It is my impression that he did not take many of his men back with him.

Perhaps the most important visit made by any orchestral society was that of Jullien, in 1853, who brought with him from forty-five to fifty men.

Jullien was a versatile genius, and in all respects a very remarkable man. His ability as a soloist on many instruments was extraordinary. I remember hearing him, when I was a boy, in Manchester, England, perform solos on the violin, piccolo, althorn, French horn, cornet, and trombone,—one instrument after the other,—displaying virtuosity on each. He was well known to be a fine violinist, which means that he must have had a natural bent for music; and he had given to it the usual slavish devotion—without which, dear admirer of the violin, do not expect to be anything of a player yourself, or to hear a player worth listening to.

MARIE BARNA. *Page* 238

The French horn is a very fascinating instrument, but it is an extremely difficult thing to attain anything like a mastery of it. The man who plays it well can easily master a cornet or althorn. The trombone is also difficult, but it is a case of family connection; and when you have been thoroughly introduced to one member, the brothers, sisters, and cousins stand with outstretched hand, ready to be wooed. The piccolo needs practice, but with the right kind of lips and a year's study, any clever musician will be enabled to astonish an ordinary audience.

According to the current history of his day, Jullien had been an officer in the French army, and was obliged to leave his country on account of the inevitable duel. How often they happen, and how convenient for public characters that the chroniclers of the same are so handy! It immediately arouses admiration to have fought a duel on account of a woman, and though never a scratch is received, it is bound to awaken a good deal of interest in the public. Jullien, according to report, had to leave France. He took refuge in England, played his musical abilities as trumps, and won every game.

This bold, venturesome character discerned

with rare acuteness the musical needs of the London metropolis, which up to his time had had no concerts but those given by the old societies, which performed classic and ancient music only, and that doubtless in "old-fogy" style.

Jullien saw his chance, gathered together a large orchestra, mainly of virtuosi on their respective instruments, and gave promenade concerts at one shilling. The plan was thoroughly successful. For years he carried all by storm. He gave monster concerts in Covent Garden or Drury Lane Theatre with immense orchestras and military bands. He made and lost fortunes; but he always contrived to secure great players, and paid them generously, which was a new feature in English musical history.

He had the ability to compose stunning big things, like the Royal Irish Quadrilles, ditto Scotch, ditto English, with endless polkas, waltzes, and other dance music. He put together every extraordinary instrument which he could employ; any and every thing which would make an effective noise, from "jingling Johnnies" to church-bells, cannon, and fireworks—he used them all, and became the great popular favorite. His music arranged for the pianoforte sold all over England, every piece having his *fac-simile* autograph stamp on the lower right-hand corner, which helped to bring him in a share of the profits.

London likes great shows as well as good artistic things. Jullien was just the man for the period in which he worked, and certainly he thoroughly exploited his versatility.

He was a master hand at catching the eye as well as the ear. At times he would lay out a small fortune in decorating the stage with plants and flowers; he knew that the artistic and picturesque must never be overlooked. The English love flowers; Jullien recognized the fact. They also like well-dressed people. Jullien was a rather handsome (if showy) man, portly, full-faced, wore side-whiskers only, and always got himself up for public show " utterly regardless," wearing a " miraculous tie," an " immaculate " white vest, and a costly diamond in his expansive shirt-front. I forget whether he wore lace cuffs or not, but he always sported a broad blue ribbon across his vest, with a decoration at his throat.

He had a dais built in the centre of the orchestra, the floor of which was covered with white cloth having a gold-lace border. On the dais he had a splendid arm-chair of white and gold. When he directed, he stood up and faced the audience, his string forces being on either hand, part way between him and the audience, but leaving him in full view; and the wood and wind were on each side, with the brass in the rear. In conducting dance music or anything of a distinctly rhythmical character, he would mark the rhythm so graphically with his baton that people actually saw it at the end of his stick. They could not mistake that, if they had eyes. No one was allowed to go to sleep. When the various soli obligati were forthcoming, he would turn to the players thereof; and the audience then saw him conduct that little or big phrase, give emphasis and expression to it, and coax it out with his baton—his wizard baton—in such a way that seeing and hearing were simply one fact. Jullien did it all.

He was in truth a hard-working man. At the end of a piece he would drop down into the splendid arm-chair, mop his face, and appear to be in a state of collapse, which drew out enormous applause. Then the great man would acknowledge the homage with really graceful thanks. It was a great sight—alone worth the price of admission.

Jullien spent money like a king among musicians. He took his large band to all the prominent cities and towns in Great Britain, losing and making money by turns. With the same spirit of venturesome confidence, he brought his great orchestra to America, and with them Mlle. Anna Zerr, a world-renowned soprano singer.

The musicians were a splendid set. He had Bottesini, the Paganini of the contrabass, and Koenig, the great cornetist of the day, who could play with wonderful expression, his rendition of the *Prima Donna Waltz* being really an artistic marvel. Then there was the oboist, Lavigne, playing with exquisite tone and fine technique, who could hold a tone (it was said) all the evening by breathing through his nostrils while playing. Then there was the necromantic flautist, Reichardt, the very fine clarinetist, Wuille, and an ophicleide-player, Mr. Hughes, who drew out of his instrument a wonderfully soft, large, and mellow tone, and played with great execution. Among the first violins were the brothers Mollenhauer, who were famous as players of duets, and who finally settled in this country. In fact so large an array of virtuosi has not visited the United States since Jullien's day.

The orchestra played a fair share of classic

music, alternating with the very popular. I remember an occasion in Boston when the *andante* of Beethoven's *Second Symphony* was on their programme. By accident the parts for the players were not forthcoming; but they played it nevertheless from memory. It was not a great feat, perhaps, but it is worthy of mention, to show that they were in the routine of playing some good music; evidently that *andante* was at their fingers' ends.

It is not easy to realize how much our musical entertainments have changed for the better, except by a glance backward at those of the preceding age. Just about forty years ago a scene was enacted by an assemblage of the best musicians of the day in the city of New York which would be scarcely credible had it not been seen and heard and described to me by a friend not given to romancing on serious subjects.

Jullien with his band was performing in the Crystal Palace, built, in what was then "uptown," in imitation of the London Palace of the Great Exposition. The New York building was not so large as that, but large enough for the time and place. Phineas T. Barnum was the directing spirit, and he of course appealed to the great popular heart every time.

FRITZ GIESE.

His theory—possibly a true one at that time, and measurably born out by some facts—was that the aforesaid heart was encased in a bumpkin's body, with a childlike intelligence and a desire for entertainments of the circus order. The more fakes and side-shows the merrier. The majority of the entertainments were intended to meet that demand and that only. Hence the scene in the Palace.

Jullien was performing a piece entitled *Night* —I cannot now give the composer's name. At the beginning the audience was told, either orally or by printed notice, that there might be some startling effects, but no one need be afraid,—all would end well, etc.

It is not a difficult task to compose an effective piece to be called *Night* with the assistance of a grand orchestra as the main factor, and given an opening of quiet, monotonous tones, like Félicien David's opening to his *Desert*, a lullaby, a lover's serenade, and lots of such odds and ends, which any good man with a lively imagination can invent. At the Crystal Palace music of this sort was purring along and lulling people into reposeful security —all quiet as night should ever be—when suddenly the clang of real fire-bells was heard; people jumped from their seats; there was a big commotion; fire and flames were seen apparently bursting from the roof of the Palace; ushers were rushing about telling people to sit down, for it was a part of the performance; the big doors were swung open, and in rushed two or three fire companies with their "machines," hose, and great fire-ladders. These ladders were raised to the roof, and the firemen, in their traditional red flannel shirts and helmets, and carrying speaking-trumpets, climbed the ladders. Real water was squirted, glass was broken, cries, orders, every sort of noise concomitant of a fire was heard,—*plus* the big orchestra, which was making a fearful din, sawing and blowing *fortissimo* through every possible diminished seventh that could be raked up out of the musical scale.

It lasted long enough to make the most tremendously red-peppered musical sensation that mortal ears ever heard.

It must be understood that all the previously distributed notices were not sufficient to prevent some timid souls from being alarmed. The noise and confusion created almost a panic. Some were fainting, others bursting with laughter, the cooler ones enthusiastically admiring the well-arranged piece. Finally, the fire was put out, the firemen with their machines retired, and the orchestra artistically prepared the audience for a song of praise and thanksgiving which came in the shape of *Old Hundred*, played and sung, and joined in by the well-pleased audience. It was a *ne plus ultra* of realistic music.

Jullien, shortly after his work in the New York Crystal Palace, returned to England. His visit to America had not been financially successful,—indeed it seemed to have been his Waterloo. He did not perform much more; he had " played out his many parts." His old admirers deserted him. Financial distress and sickness overtook him, and he came to a sudden and sad ending in an insane asylum.

CHAPTER IX

IT has always been an open question whether Boston made the Handel and Haydn Society or the Handel and Haydn Society made Boston.

The Society has been almost an integral part of the city since 1815, the year of its formation. If we consider the total result,— the beneficial and wide-spread influence of the Society on the great mass of New England people,—then we can comprehend how much honor it has unvaryingly reflected on Boston.

I wish to disclaim any pretension to writing an accurate history of any Boston musical society before I was a working member of any of them. I shall only try to tell something of what they did, and how they did it, in my time.

When I was engaged to play clarinet in the Handel and Haydn Society, it was a very cosy domestic institution. I cannot say whether there was or was not a regular music conductor that first season. I remember distinctly that good old "father" Jonas Chickering did often beat time while they had their "sing." These meetings were always held (according to their By-Laws), and are still, on Sunday evenings, from the first Sunday in October to the last Sunday in May.

Like most societies of the period, the Handel and Haydn was composed of both instrumental and vocal members. Amateur players comprised about two thirds, and professionals one third, of the orchestra. The professionals were engaged to "help out." We were paid the modest sum of two dollars for each evening, whether concert or rehearsal, every Sunday through the season. It was an invaluable apprenticeship. I believe that musicians of the present day, who do not have the slow building-up through the regular performance of oratorios, lose a schooling no other music can give. Old Bostonians were great gainers by being permeated with the *Messiah*, the *Israel in Egypt, Samson, Jephtha, Solomon, Saul, Judas Maccabæus, Acis and Galatea*, and *Esther*, all by Handel; the *Creation*, the *Seasons*, and masses, by Haydn; the *Elijah, St. Paul*, and the *Hymn of Praise*, by Mendelssohn; and the *Requiem* and other masses, by Mozart.

Nor did the Society stop with the above

works. They were right catholic in their tastes. They gave operas founded on sacred histories, such as *Moses in Egypt*, by Rossini; the *Martyrs*, by Donizetti, and *Nabucco*, by Verdi. The *Moses* had a popular run for several seasons. Rossini was then in vogue. Indeed the great arias with their quite tremendous instrumental solo introductions, and the effective concerted pieces and *finales* of dramatic energy, would be startling even at the present day.

Time brought changes. The amateur players dropped off. The " Profs " were released from Sunday attendance. The Society began to engage orchestras of professional players for a definite number of concerts only.

Various conductors have contributed their share towards the musical development of the Society.

Mr. Charles Horn, the English song-writer, was, I believe, imported in order to bring out the oratorio of *Elijah*. I think he was followed by John L. Hatton. This gentleman was a very fine musician and composer, an excellent pianist, and, *mirable dictu*, an exceptionally fine, unctuous singer of comic songs.

Think of it, classicists of the present day,— the director of the Handel and Haydn Society a famous singer of comic songs! I can assure my readers, though, that when Mr. Hatton sang *The Little Fat Man, Bluebeard,* or *The Jolly Young Oysterman* (words by Oliver Wendell Holmes, music by Hatton), he satisfied very largely the æsthetic tastes of the day. It is also to be remembered that there are comic songs and comic songs. Those Mr. Hatton sang were distinctly musical, with piano accompaniments like those by Franz or Grieg.

Mr. Hatton's versatility was great. I remember an instance of it. One Saturday night in a Musical Fund concert, he played Mendelssohn's *D-Minor Piano Concerto,*—that being its first performance in Boston. Later, in the same concert, he sang some comic songs. The next evening, in the same hall, in a Handel and Haydn concert, he conducted a performance of the *Elijah.* The singer of the title *rôle* was suddenly indisposed and unable to sing. Mr. Hatton, through the entire performance, sang the part of "Elijah,"—turning around to face the audience when singing, yet continuing to conduct the forces. He sang the music in artistic style and with a good, full voice.

Mr. Hatton stayed in Boston about two seasons, and was a splendid worker in the musical life of the city.

There was a Mr. Davidson, who conducted for part of a season only. He was followed by Mr. Charles C. Perkins, who filled the office of conductor and president of the society for several years. Mr. Perkins was a devoted patron of music, and indeed of all the fine arts. He was of the true *noblesse*, almost un-American in his patrician-like devotion to and working for the advancement of art. A graduate of Harvard, he had spent some years in Europe studying music and painting. Returning to Boston, he mingled actively in the musical life of the city, and for years he had a musical evening at his house each week. Chamber music by the Mendelssohn Quintette Club and our best local or visiting pianists did good service then and there by familiarizing devotees of music with excerpts of the best kind. At Mr. Perkins's house was heard for the first time Schumann's *Piano Qnintette*, with Mr. William Scharfenberg (recently deceased) at the piano. I remember the occurrence well. We young artists were so stirred up and excited by the *Quintette* that when we ended its last note we simply turned our parts back again to the beginning and played the whole work once more, *con amore*.

Mr. Perkins was a zealous worker for the

CARL ZERRAHN.

building of the Boston Music Hall; and he did himself and the city of Boston honor by presenting to the Hall the splendid bronze statue of Beethoven, by Crawford, the sculptor. Later on he was an equally ardent worker for the building and founding of the Art Museum; and for years he devoted much time to teaching and lecturing on art subjects in the Normal School. He was a fairly good pianist, and had composed a number of pieces of chamber music, —trios, quartettes, and a septette for piano and strings. Wherever his money, labor, or influence could reach, they were actively employed for the advancement of art. And since his tragic death, no one has stepped forward to quite take his place.

The next conductor and pilot of the society was Mr. Carl Zerrahn, who was for many years at the helm. Advanced age alone induced him, at the beginning of the season of 1895, to retire from his responsible position.

Taking Mr. Zerrahn in all points, he was and is still a rare man. He has filled a long life with honor to himself and satisfaction to those who came in contact with him. First showing good ability as the director of the Orchestral Union, he afterward became the conductor of the Harvard Symphony Concerts, the

Handel and Haydn Society, and the Worcester Festivals. He was always much in demand in New England, and in fact from Maine to California. He possessed one trait of character which manifested itself during the laborious working of a music festival.

Let us suppose that the festival began at 9 A.M. on Monday, and continued with rehearsals or performances till Saturday night: I can testify, from personal experience while assisting in the festivals, that Mr. Zerrahn was always as fresh, as full of interest, and as energetic at the last hour as he was at the first. In that particular trait, which every musician knows to be an important one, he was a matchless man.

He was also very firm and earnest in action, amiable in temper, and considerate of the shortcomings of the many inexperienced performers who came under his baton. He was never known to show up the weakness of an artist to the public; neither the highest nor the humblest assistant ever received a discourteous word from him. He was and is still a rare man indeed; and unquestionably is enthroned in the hearts of very large numbers of those who came under his direction.

Another man worthy of being singled out is Dr. J. P. Upham, for many years president of the Handel and Haydn Society, who as an executive officer and organizer was quite Napoleonic. It was mainly through his labors that sufficient interest was aroused to purchase the great organ for the Music Hall. His master work in Boston, however, was in creating a strong popular belief in the benefits arising from the teaching of music in the public schools, and in the further wisdom of holding a yearly exhibition, in the shape of a School Music Festival, to show the total results thereof.

I cannot end my friendly record of the Handel and Haydn Society without mentioning the untiring service of the two "war secretaries," Loring B. Barnes and J. Parker Brown. The latter has also been for many years the president of the society. Every man of experience in the management of societies knows that there are times when much zeal and tact, personal influence, and unceasing vigilance, alone "keep the machine running." Those are the qualities which win victory from threatening defeat. Mr. Barnes and Mr. Brown have merited great praise for the forethought and foresight displayed while engaging the array of artists for the many Handel and Haydn Festivals; they were doubtless inspired by

Santa Cecilia, the sweet patroness of music, to make the sacrifices on her altars so willingly performed by all her devotees.

Mr. B. J. Lang, the almost lifelong organist and steadfast helper of the Handel and Haydn Society, and for a time the successor of Carl Zerrahn as conductor, has shown in countless ways such consummate skill, tact, and artistic judgment that he has won the admiration of all musicians. He is a man of marked character, a typical American, ambitious and industrious. I have known him since his boyhood, when he lived with his parents in their quiet home in Salem, Mass. I used to meet him frequently on the train for Boston, where he went to take piano or organ lessons, and I noticed that he prepared his harmony lessons while *en route*. In this way the youth grew up, systematically laying the foundation for his future usefulness. Now at maturity he has the reputation of being a distinguished pianist, organist, teacher, and general director. A few sentences will suffice to outline the life of the busy artist since he made his *début* at fifteen years of age in one of the Mendelssohn Quintette Club's concerts.

Mr. Lang has always been a hard student, and is known by his friends to be a progres-

B. J. LANG.

sive man, with many new and bright ideas. While still very young he organized, in 1862, a couple of concerts, in which he appeared as the conductor of a large orchestra, chorus, and soloists, in two performances of the *Walpurgis Nacht*. He thus entered upon a broad, artistic life, and has continued in the same path. He has been the conductor of the Apollo Club since its formation in 1871, and also of the St. Cecilia Club. The first concert of the latter was given November 19, 1874, orchestra assisting. The programme consisted of several part-songs and the *Walpurgis Nacht*, by Mendelssohn. One of the most notable accomplishments of Mr. Lang was the bringing out of the *Passion-Play* of *Parsifal* by Richard Wagner. At great expense he brought from New York the entire Seidl Orchestra, which had recently played the work in that city. It was a bold and brilliant stroke. No other performance of the great composition has been vouchsafed Boston.

It is a great pleasure to be able to give a slight sketch of his daughter, Margaret Ruthven Lang. She was born in 1867, and inherits the musical ability of her parents. Her mother is well known as an amateur singer of great refinement. Miss Lang, therefore, has had a musical education which has been carefully directed in every detail. She has attained a position which places her among the four foremost female composers of the world, the other three being Chaminade and Holmes of Paris, and Mrs. Beach of Boston.

Miss Lang began writing music when about twelve years old. Among her first compositions were a quintette of one movement for strings and piano, and several songs. She began the study of the pianoforte under one of her father's pupils, and later continued it under his direction. Some time after this she studied the violin with Louis Schmidt in Boston, and continued it under Drechsler and Abel, in Munich, during the winters of 1886–1887. While in Munich she also studied composition with Victor Gluth.

On returning to Boston in 1887, she took up the study of orchestration with G. W. Chadwick, since which time she has written a large number of compositions, many of which have had great success.

Her *Dramatic Overture, op.* 12, was performed by the Boston Symphony Orchestra, under Nikisch, on April 8, 1893; her overture *Witichis, op.* 10, was performed in Chicago under Theodore Thomas, at two concerts, in

July and August, 1893; and at a third concert under Bendix. Both of these compositions are in manuscript; also a third overture, *op.* 23, *Totila*. Of other works for orchestra, composed later, are three arias: one for alto, *Sappho's Prayer to Aphrodite*, performed in New York in 1896; one for soprano, *Armida*, performed at the Boston Symphony Concert, January 13, 1896; and one for baritone, *Phœbus*.

CHAPTER X

AMONG the many artists with whom I have come in contact, none had a personality which made a greater impression on me than Ole Bull. His magnificent figure, that head of long hair and the way he had of throwing it back to keep it out of his eyes when performing, made a picture which memory easily retains. His career as a virtuoso in America and Europe is too well known to require much mention of it here.

The question has often been put to me: What kind of an artist was Ole Bull? It was a question difficult to answer, and I tried to follow the example of wise men, and diplomatically evade giving a musical opinion. I shall use the same tactics now. There are a few points, though, that I have never seen brought out in any criticism.

The apothegm of President Lincoln, "You can't fool all the people all the time," comes into play in this case. There were many reasons for Ole Bull's great popularity. He had some remarkable points in technique; for instance, his marvelous *staccato;* also his trick of playing a four-part harmony on an almost flat bridge. His rendition of *The Mother's Prayer* was a finished performance, while that of *The Arkansas Traveller* was simply a stroke of genius in its way.

A poor way, the musician will say. Of course it was, but it was a way by which he gained great popularity. I heard him play *The Arkansas Traveller* once; I shall never forget it. The piece opened with a short introduction,—a quiet, plaintive air,—at the conclusion of which he gently lifted up his right foot, much in the old-grandfather manner of beating time; then he suddenly brought down that foot with tremendous force on the uncarpeted stage and dashed off into the most reckless, mad, and intoxicated jig any dancer ever heard to start the fever of dancing within him. It was startling.

Our Quintette Club was engaged to play with Ole Bull for a week. He was requested to play first violin in one of Mozart's quintettes,— a first movement only. We had to stand up while playing it. To sit down and play was an impossibility for the heroic Ole. At the time of the first Jubilee in Boston, he and Carl Rosa played at the first desk of violins. We all thought it noble of him to take part.

Ole Bull had all the fine traits of the successful player. After each of his performances there was usually great applause. When he came out on the stage to acknowledge the compliment, his manner was so uncommonly graceful, so stately-courteous, as he bowed right and left, that the audience was, if possible, more completely captured than when he was playing to them.

Ole Bull visited the United States for the first time in 1843. He returned to Europe, but revisited America many times. He had great happiness in the last part of his life, resulting from his marriage with an American woman of unusual distinction of character. He died in the home he had created for his family on a picturesque island in one of Norway's wonderful fjords.

Boston had another remarkable man to help in the building up of a refined taste for music,—Julius Eichberg.

Mr. Eichberg came to this country in 1847, and was in New York for two years. In 1849 he removed to Boston, and was appointed director of music in the Boston Museum. While in that position he composed and pro-

OLE BULL.

duced several operettas of charming quality, notably the *Doctor of Alcantara*, though as a composer he was academic. In that vein he wrote a good quintette for strings, which was played by our Club; also a concerto for four violins, which was performed at a benefit concert for the Musical Union.

In 1867 he established the Boston Conservatory of Music, which was chiefly a violin school of great value, and which is still at work, under the direction of Mr. Herbert P. Chelius. Mr. Eichberg was a fine violinist and a man of culture. He was thoroughly appreciated in our community, and was for many years the general supervisor and director of music for all the high schools of Boston, in which capacity he did good work for the people of the "Modern Athens."

CHAPTER XI

THE Mendelssohn Quintette Club may be said to be like Topsy,—"not born but just growed."

The members of the Club were:

August Fries, 1st violin; Francis Riha, 2d violin; Edward Lehman, viola and flute; Thomas Ryan, viola and clarinet; Wulf Fries, violoncello.

Its real career began with its first public concert in Boston, December, 1849.

This was the programme:

1. QUINTETTE IN A, OP. 18 . . . *Mendelssohn.*
   Four Movements.
2. LA MELANCOLIE, solo for violin . . *Prume.*
   MR. FRANCIS RIHA.
3. TRIO FOR FLUTE, VIOLIN, AND VIOLONCELLO, on themes from the opera of "Zampa," by Hérold.
   Kalliwoda.
   MESSRS. LEHMAN, AUGUST AND WULF FRIES.
4. FIFTH AIR VARIÉ FOR CLARINET. . . *F. Berr.*
   MR. THOMAS RYAN.
5. QUINTETTE IN E FLAT, OP. 4 . . *Beethoven.*
   Four Movements.

That programme was certainly a notable one—fit for to-day's use. We had set our standard high; and have never lowered it during our almost fifty years of service.

The custom of the period, which prohibited theatrical performances Saturdays, gave the musicians entire freedom on those days. Mr. August Fries and his brother Wulf, members of the National Theatre Orchestra, were devoted quartette players, and they always utilized their precious freedom on Saturdays by getting their *confrères* together to play quartettes with them. In this way the foundation was laid for the formation of the Quintette Club. The Fries brothers enlisted the interest of Messrs. Gierlow, Greuner, and Lehman. These five began to play for their own enjoyment, and after a while they played at a few concerts outside of Boston before I was a member.

In 1849, Mr. August Fries gave violin lessons to Mr. John Bigelow, of the well-known firm, Bigelow Brothers & Kennard, jewellers. By invitation of Mr. Bigelow these five artists spent many of their Saturday evenings at his house. Having the pleasure of Mr. Bigelow's acquaintance, I also was at his house on most of these occasions and to use the common expression, it made me "just crazy" to play with them.

One day I said in jest to August Fries, "You'll do nothing till I am a member of the Mendelssohn Quintette Club." Shortly after, one of the gentlemen, Mr. Greuner, removed to Lowell, and I was invited to take his place. Then Mr. Gierlow resigned, and Francis Riha, the former leader of the Steyermark Orchestra, took his place and thus became the second violin. We played very much together and got into fine trim.

Mr. Bigelow, who was our fatherly friend, and remained such all through life, suggested that we should prepare to give concerts, and make that a part of our life-work. The question of a name naturally came up. Mendelssohn was on the top of the musical wave at that time, and, as we had practised his quintette, *Opus* 18, till we could venture to play it in public, it was determined to call our party, The Mendelssohn Quintette Club of Boston. We gave our first concert by invitation, in Jonas Chickering's piano rooms, then on Washington Street, nearly opposite the Adams House.

Framed under glass in my home, I have one of the little modest notes of invitation to that

THE MENDELSSOHN QUINTETTE CLUB.

concert, sent to about two hundred people; also the little yellow tissue-paper programme, three inches by five, printed for the memorable occasion.

We jumped into favor at once, gave a set of four subscription concerts, and afterward a supplementary set in old Cochituate Hall (Phillips Place), where now is Houghton & Dutton's store.

Then for us young men began a kind of belle's life. We were in demand everywhere,—not only for single concerts, but for sets of four or more,—in places like Salem, Lowell, Lawrence, Haverhill, Taunton, New Bedford, Providence, and Worcester. Concerts, in sets, were usually held once a fortnight.

There were no dramatic or operatic companies to visit such places; but the lyceum system was well established everywhere. Each town and city had its organized sets of lectures. In Boston there were two library associations that were rivals; and the astutest generalship was displayed in capturing the great lecture guns of the day,—Wendell Phillips, Geo. W. Curtis, Mr. Whipple, Mr. Agassiz, and others. It is recorded that the president of one of these societies, calling on Mr. Agassiz at a period when he was working enthusiastically on one of his books, laid down before Mr. Agassiz a blank check, duly signed, that the latter could fill out to any amount for a lecture. Mr. Agassiz simply said that his time was "too precious," he could "not afford to work for money." Those were the halcyon days of the lecture field.

In order to appreciate the environment of the Quintette Club during our early years, we have but to remember that Boston, within a radius of one hundred miles, had a very large number of towns and cities of active working communities. With the exception of a few places like Providence, Worcester, and Portland, these towns had no theatres; their only entertainments were lectures or concerts, and these were mostly given in churches; so we had all New England to ourselves (as far as supplying music was concerned) for many years.

Parlor concerts were in vogue. In Cambridge, for instance, we had for fifteen consecutive seasons a set of eight parlor concerts, given in the houses of the professors or other friends of music. The programmes were of good music only. We also had for years sets of parlor concerts in places like Milton and New Bedford.

In this same period the "Yankee singing-school" and the so-called "musical conventions" flourished. The latter were held for years in Maine, New Hampshire, Vermont, and Massachusetts. The singers of these different States had organized governing boards that appointed the time of meeting and engaged the music director and assisting artists. The chorus of singers chiefly studied so-called "sacred music," and usually wound up their week's labor with an oratorio performance.

The members of the "musical conventions" usually began their rehearsals on Monday at nine A.M., and continued till noon. The afternoon session was from two to four, and was largely given up to solo singing or playing by our Club. It also afforded an opportunity for the amateurs of the State to display their ability in public. Many of the young singers afterward became noted in the musical world. Among them was Annie Louise Cary, who acquired a European operatic reputation that placed her in the front rank among great singers. From this kind of training, too, came Mrs. H. M. Smith, Mrs. Mozart, Jenny Kempton, Myron Whitney, James Whitney (tenor), and a host of others too numerous to mention.

The evenings of the conventions were generally devoted to mixed music, in which the chorus took part. Nearly every oratorio worthy of mention—entire or in part—was thus familiarized to people who lived in the remotest parts of New England.

This little history will account for the possibility of assembling, on occasions like the Gilmore Peace Jubilees, a chorus numbering five to ten thousand singers who were at home in oratorio music. Outside of New England no similar condition existed.

The singing-school and the musical conventions no longer command the same popular interest, for which various reasons can be adduced. The main one is the fact that entertainments and *professional entertainers* of all kinds have multiplied. The people prefer seeing the game of baseball played by experts to playing the game themselves. The same thing is true of the people's enjoyment of music.

Whatever be the cause, we know that in towns and small cities, the old music societies have generally ceased to exist. The singing-school teachers who began in New England are now scattered over the West. They have carried with them their old home ways; for instance, Mr. Amos Whiting, formerly of Worcester, Mass., who removed to Pittsburg, Pa., and at once began work on the old singing-school and convention plan. In a few years he roused enough interest in that community to project and carry through a magnificent festival, in which Madame Nilsson and her troupe of singers took part in an oratorio. Mrs. Whiting has been doing the same thing in Toledo, Ohio. I could mention other teachers, but the instances given are fair types of the fraternity.

While on the subject of musical conventions and New England singers, I wish to interject a remark,—not as a compliment on the one hand, nor as a defamation on the other,—namely: in the conventions it was often the case that Rossini's *Stabat Mater* was performed, and I can aver that the most perfect singing of the two quartettes (concerted) in that work was often done by Mrs. H. M. Smith, soprano; Miss Annie Louise Cary, alto; Mr. James Whitney, tenor; Mr. Myron Whitney, bass. The intonation of those singers was as positively perfect as any musician could desire to hear.

In contradistinction, I think no musician can speak favorably of the performance of the same works by any combination of so-called great or distinguished artists that he has since heard in the United States. The reasons are not far to seek. The so-called "great" people generally are only good in solo work, where they can "shine!" They do not, they will not, sacrifice their individual art to ensure a good *ensemble*. They never, for the sake of the true rendition of these quartettes, so chromatically difficult, are willing to rehearse them till they are fairly perfect. They, the artists, must be considered before the music.

Our home-bred singers were not made on that pattern—they strove for perfection, and very nearly reached it. At least that is my opinion, and I here put it on record. "Let justice be done though the heavens fall."

ANNIE LOUISE CARY.

CHAPTER XII

AMONG the singers who about twenty years ago gained American and European celebrity, easily stands pre-eminent Annie Louise Cary, now Mme. Raymond. As a contralto singer, in concert, oratorio, or opera, she won all hearts with her superb voice and expressive vocalization. A native of the State of Maine,—born and reared near Portland,—she has in many ways shown a filial love for her State and endeared herself, one may say forever, to its people.

When she was at the height of her professional glory, she fitted up at her own expense a "Cary Room" in the Maine General Hospital, and that room is to be kept up at her expense to the end of her days. That is an act I deem worthy to be placed on record, and I hope it may often be imitated. Yet it is but one of the many good acts of the brave American girl.

To return to the history of the Mendelssohn

Club, we were by no means paddling our own little Quintette "canoe" only, but were active members of the different orchestras of the Musical Fund, the Orchestral Union, the Harvard Association, and the Boston Symphony, each in turn as they came into action.

The Orchestral Union was made up from our best musicians,—about forty in number,—Carl Zerrahn being the director. The concerts were held in Music Hall on Wednesday afternoons only. The entrance fee was moderate. Programmes were of mixed music: an overture, symphony, waltz, characteristic pieces, and opera selections. The great organ in Music Hall was built about the time the Union began their concerts. Our best organists were invited in turn to play organ solos at each concert. The Union existed about ten years, then ended its life for lack of support.

The friends of symphonic music, hungering for the best in quality, organized in 1865 the Harvard Musical Association. Mr. Carl Zerrahn was engaged as conductor, and, with an efficient orchestra, gave programmes of symphonic music. In the first three years, eight concerts were given each season; then for ten seasons, ten concerts. The number was reduced to eight for the next three seasons, and in the last season but five were given; making in all seventeen seasons. The programmes were worthy models for any society which means to be educative; to interest the best-music lovers, and yet to remember the large army of those who desire the simplest sort of music. Finally, in spite of the wisdom exercised by the directors, interest in the concerts waned and they ended.

In 1880 the worthy benefactor, Mr. Henry L. Higginson, founded the Boston Symphony Orchestra. That orchestra has made its own record, which is simply one of increasing perfection. It is now perhaps the model orchestra of the world; and every good citizen of Boston has reason to be proud of the honors it wins for its founder and the city of its birth.

Up to the year 1863, when the Quintette Club first travelled in the West, we gave each year eight subscription concerts in Boston. The old friends and supporters remained faithful to us, and were part of our glory. Their faces and names rise before me as I write.

First, there is our good old father, John Bigelow, who with his family nearly always sat in the front seats. Mr. Bigelow was an inspiration. He had a pair of hands of generous proportions, and when he applauded the house went with him. When he was not present, it was comparatively a dull night. One may talk of horses sniffing the smoke of battle, but it is a faint figure of speech compared to the sniffing of artists for applause. It is whip and spur to them.

In these classic soirées of ours, we have played every composition for strings worth playing; and have given also special sets of concerts where only the most modern works, like the Brahms sextettes, Bruch, Goldmark, and Rubinstein, were played. We also gave for many seasons the so-called popular Saturday night concerts; for which we secured other artists to play septettes, octettes, and nonettes of mixed wind and string instruments. Nearly every pianist of distinction played repeatedly with us; among them were Mr. William Scharfenberg, Otto Dresel, Ernst Perabo, J. C. D. Parker, B. J. Lang, Hugo Leonard, Gustav Satter, J. Trenkle, John L. Hatton, and Miss Fay (now Mrs. Sherwood).

Singers also helped us in large numbers. One was Mlle. Caroline Lehman, sister of our flute player, who came from Copenhagen and sang with us two seasons. Other vocal assistants were Mrs. J. H. Long, Mrs. Went-

MR. JOHN BIGELOW.

worth, Mrs. Harwood, Miss Addie S. Ryan, Mrs. H. M. Smith, Adelaide Phillips, and Annie Louise Cary—all good singers. I think it can be safely said that the Mendelssohn Quintette Club has done its share in cultivating a taste for music, especially chamber music.

It is next in order to tell my readers something of the musical and personal qualities of the members of the Mendelssohn Quintette Club.

Naturally I begin with August Fries. He was a good, genuine violinist, especially in quartette. He played with deep sentiment, was painstaking, and no rehearsals were too long for him. He was the broadest man, had the oldest head, of the organization, and was altogether a good leader. In his social character he was full of geniality, could be the life and spirit of every party, and he thus endeared himself to a very large number of personal friends. He had the old-world habit (a charming one) of studying beforehand how a social evening could be most pleasantly spent. It was always clear to his friends that he had interested himself to plan for their pleasure. That fact was the key to his character,—he accustomed himself to think of others. Whether it was a picnic, sail, dance, or musical evening, he was the leader in it all. He was very firm in purpose and set in his way; he could not accommodate himself to some things; but sterling integrity was the main point in his make-up. He was an excellent man for younger people to start with.

August Fries stayed with us ten years. He then returned to Bergen, in Norway, where he has lived ever since, with the exception of a visit to Boston about twenty years ago, when for one season he filled the post of concertmaster with the Harvard Association.

Mr. Wulf Fries, brother to August, was and is a good 'cellist. He is so well known throughout the country that eulogistic words from me are unnecessary. It is not easy to find a 'cellist for all general playing who produces a tone comparable to that of Fries; and we have had in the Club some of the best 'cellists of this country,—namely: Fries for twenty-two years; the splendid 'cellist, Rudolph Hennig, of Philadelphia, for eight years; Giese, a great player, for four or five years; and Hekking for one year. For certain work and tone, Fries was up to the level of them all. His personal friends can be counted in legions.

Mr. Francis Riha, our second violin, was a brilliant player in every way, with considerable ability as a composer. He was the handsome man of the party,—much petted but not spoiled. He stayed with us five years, and then went south for a milder climate, but returned to New York when the war began.

Edward Lehman, a good flute and viola player, stayed with us four years, and then returned to Copenhagen, where he was the solo flute with Lumbye for years.

CHAPTER XIII

NOW is the time to ask, in the words of the old song, "Where are the friends of my youth?" They are scattered like the leaves of past autumns; but the memory of many of them remains as a rich inheritance.

One of the noblest of the band was "old Jonas Chickering." In fancy I can see him now in his workshop in the big factory on Washington Street. He was a medium-sized man with a most kindly face. When at work he wore a white linen apron, and naturally was "in his shirt-sleeves." His special task was to cover all the hammers for his best pianofortes with buckskin,—an important thing in those days, before the invention of the white felt now used; which comes, so to speak, ready-made to glue on to the hammers from bass to soprano. Mr. Chickering could be generally found with a sharp knife in hand preparing the hammers. If customers called, ladies or gentlemen, he simply put down his knife and waited on them; that was the old style.

He had taken a fatherly interest in me, and I frequently found myself in his den, telling him my dreams and aspirations; and I know other young musicians who were often with him. He liked their chatter, and exchanged good counsel for it. It was a way he had. From the time that our Quintette Club gave its first concert in his rooms, he was a great help and generous subscriber.

One day I said to him, "Mr. Chickering, you are everlastingly doing much for us,—cannot we do something for you? For instance, it would be a great pleasure if we could give you a musical evening at your house." He smiled, thanked me, and said perhaps he would have one. Months after, he arranged for the evening and we greatly enjoyed it. Some little time passed by. I went into his den one day, and had my usual chat with him. When I was about to leave he said, "By the way, Mr. Ryan, Mr. Childs, the bookkeeper, wishes to see you." I saw Mr. Childs, and he handed me a check for fifty dollars. To cut my story short, there was no use in protesting; Mr. Chickering insisted on my taking the money. That was the style of the "upright," "square," "grand" old man.

I am sure that this incident is but a sample

of the way in which he helped many young musicians; and it is an open secret that the father's ways were inherited by his noble sons, of whom George only is living.

When I speak of Mr. Jonas Chickering, the head of the great house, working and waiting on ladies in his shirt-sleeves, all people of my age will understand it without mental question or comment. It will not be so well understood by people of the present day, who, almost to the verge of the absurd, feel that they must not be visible except in full dress; to be seen working with an apron on would be to voluntarily place themselves in a humbler (to use soft words) stratum of society.

But let me tell you, boys, what was done once by the man who wore the white linen apron. One sad night, his great factory on Washington Street was burned down. At daylight on the following morning a contract was signed, purchasing a lot of land on Tremont Street, and within twenty-four hours the building of another great factory was started. It has been, and is, a noble pile,—that workshop and factory of the Chickerings. I think great credit is due to the man who had so much foresight as to place his factory where the city would grow to it. Mr. Chickering

JONAS CHICKERING.

was at that time the honored president of the Mechanics' Charitable Association. His history ought to encourage young men to wear white linen aprons, if necessary, without fear or shame.

The next good old friend who rises into memory is Mr. Thomas Power, the clerk of the police court for many years. He was a curious mixture. In his official routine he was a terror to evil-doers; the presiding judge was of little account in comparison. When Mr. Power revealed the depravity of the "he" or "she" under arrest, and the number of times he or she had already been up before his Honor, and the long list of broken promises to reform, there was a something in the tone of his voice which distinctly implied, not only grief, but utter absence of hope that people of that kind would ever obtain a foothold in the good part of the next world. It then became a case of "Who enters here leaves hope behind," for the culprit was shortly sentenced to three or six months in jail.

Mr. Power, when thus officially employed, was the most "solemncholy" man I ever met. But out of the court room he was a really genial soul, the prince of good fellows, a famous story-teller, and positively a lovable man.

I recall one of his queer stories. He had been authorized by his Honor, the judge, to obtain a legal opinion on a certain point from the Hon. Rufus Choate. Mr. Choate's chirography was notoriously the worst ever seen, and must have been like that made by the traditional fly when it crawled out of the inkbottle into which it had accidentally fallen. The opinion was obtained, and was in Mr. Choate's characteristic handwriting. Poor "Tom Power" looked at it, as he said, "upside down, right side up, and crosswise," but it was not possible for him to read it in any position. He then went over to Mr. Joseph Bell, Mr. Choate's partner, and got him to write it out. Armed with both writings, Mr. Power went to court, and the case was called. Being asked to read Mr. Choate's opinion, he took up the (Bell) paper, read it glibly, and laid it on his desk. His Honor asked to see the document. Mr. Power obligingly handed Mr. Choate's letter up to him. The judge looked at it with wondering eyes, then at Mr. Power, and finally, drawing a long breath, he asked Mr. Power how it was possible for him to read it.

"Oh," said Mr. Power, "it happens to be one of my accomplishments!"

LOWELL MASON.

I have evidence of Mr. Power's kindly disposition toward our Club in the form of a letter in his handwriting. I have had it framed, and I hold it in veneration.

"BOSTON, March 31, 1852.
" *To the Members of the Mendelssohn Quintette Club:*

"GENTLEMEN:—Holding in regard your position as artists, we offer you a complimentary benefit. If you accept this offer, please name an evening when it will be convenient to you.

"With sentiments of regard,
"SAMUEL A. ELIOT,
THOMAS POWER,
JOSEPH BELL,
G. CUSHING,
JOHN BIGELOW,
HENRY BURDITT,
WM. B. COFFIN,
DANIEL KIMBALL, JR.,
RUFUS CHOATE,
JAMES LODGE,
FRANKLIN DARRACOTT,
JONAS CHICKERING."

To a Bostonian these are names which carry weight and social distinction. Of these twelve gentlemen not one is now alive.

The concert held in response to the above request, was one of the occasions which will ever remain a precious memory to the Club. Especially charming is the souvenir of that little girl who, advancing to the stage, placed in the hands of each of our number a bouquet, to which was attached a note of thanks and a substantial token of regard in the shape of a valuable gold ring and a large gold piece.

I also hold as a treasure one of our old subscription lists, well filled with names. I read the paper from top to bottom; I know every name, recall every person (about two hundred), and know they were always to be counted on. They were the friends of our youth, and now are mostly with the autumn leaves.

> " Many a time and oft,
> When the house is still and the day is done
> And the stars are out aloft,
> I sit by the failing fire alone
> And think of the years that are past and gone—
> Many a time and oft." [1]
>
> [1] Amelia B. Edwards.

CHAPTER XIV

THE next old friend who looms up large is Mr. Lowell Mason—a prominent figure in the musical history of the United States. I believe he was never absent from any of our chamber concerts except when out of town. I well remember how, one night in the old Masonic Temple, when we had finished playing Mendelssohn's Quartette in D, *op.* 44, Mr. Mason rose from his seat in the second row, came to the stage, laid the score of the quartette at my feet, said, "It was beautifully played; please keep the score; sorry I cannot stay longer," and walked out in the stately, self-possessed manner so perfectly in keeping with his character.

At his home on Kingston Street I first met his sons, William and Henry. William, as we well know, is one of the foremost of American musicians, a splendid pianist and composer for the pianoforte. The youngest brother, Henry, also had musical talent. He became the head of the firm of Mason & Hamlin, the reed-organ builders, and latterly grand and upright piano makers. There were two elder brothers,— Lowell and Daniel; not being of my age, I knew them very little. They became well-known business men in New York City.

Mr. Oliver Ditson is another well-known figure in musical history. He has so recently left his "niche," as one may properly call it, in his store, that it is easy to think he will return to it in a minute or so. Mr. Ditson never wanted more than standing-room for his own working-place; he always stood when writing. He had all the old-style habits, —was at his desk from 9 A.M. till 2 P.M. at all seasons of the year, and never went so far from Boston in the summer that he could not come to his store daily for work.

Mr. Ditson was an actively benevolent man. It is well known that he paid the expenses of several music students, enabling them to study in Europe. His more private benefactions will never be known, but they are guessed at by his friends. His methodical habits and practical ways of economizing time were strong traits in his character; they would often "crop out" in a funny manner, and a little story may serve to illustrate these peculiarities.

Mr. Ditson had been out for a drive; the

OLIVER DITSON.

horses had bolted, the vehicle was wrecked, Mr. Ditson was thrown out, his left arm was dislocated, and his whole body badly bruised. He was picked up, and surgical assistance put him measurably to rights; but he was forced to keep his room for perhaps four days,—a long time to be absent from duty. Finally he returned to his niche, with his arm in a sling, and joyfully resumed work. I was in Vermont at the time of the accident, but read all about it in the newspapers. Returning to the city, I hastened to learn Mr. Ditson's condition. There he was in his old niche, large as life, but a little damaged about the head, with his arm in a sling. Full of personal sympathy, I asked him to tell me all about the accident. Without interrupting his writing for more than a second, he handed me a sheet of paper on which he had written a full history of the occurrence. It was entirely unnecessary to ask a single question. I offered my condolences, which he received with warm thanks, and took my leave.

We must not overlook the fact that the great music house of Ditson & Co. remains with us as a truly magnificent monument to the name of Oliver Ditson. It is one to which every citizen of Boston can point with pride;

and as a music-publishing house is one of the largest in the world. Mr. Ditson, like the majority of America's great merchants, had his "day of small beginnings." His native wisdom served him to very good purpose. It was but natural that he looked with honest pride on his son Charles controlling a great Ditson house in New York City, and his youngest son, Edward (when alive), doing the same thing in Philadelphia.

I must not close this section of my recollections without recalling the well-known prince of musical editors,—John Sebastian Dwight. His kindly face and form, so well known to Boston people, have so recently left us that we simply think that the good man has just gone away for a little while on a journey, and that we shall certainly see him again in his old haunts. We get so accustomed to see certain people in certain places, year in and year out, that we expect to see them there always. We were so sure of seeing Mr. Dwight in his invariable, carefully selected seat in the left-hand side of the first balcony of Music Hall, that now, missing him from that seat, one naturally asks, "Where is John S. to-night?" In this way beneficent nature lets the recollections of our dearest friends slowly fade out into the illimitable confines of memory.

When Mr. Dwight began to publish his weekly paper, *Dwight's Journal of Music*, in 1852, it was pioneer work—uphill ploughing and planting. John S. was ahead of his time in his requirements from public performers. He was to us young fellows, and indeed to all artists, at once a spur and a whip. He would never compromise with anything mean or common in music, and was peculiarly intolerant of anything of the "monster jubilee" order. From his standpoint he was right. He had the courage of his convictions, and was willing to risk going without salt for his porridge rather than support in his paper any work which did not possess the element of refined merit.

At the time of the Boston Jubilees, which were big popular affairs, very wonderful in their way, with an army of guarantors for their financial success, the people, in Mr. Dwight's opinion, were largely guarantors for business reasons only. That was sufficient to draw out his strongest opposition; he could not tolerate the Jubilees.

Among the guarantors was the noble, large-hearted Mr. Oliver S. Ditson. He naturally wished for the influence of Mr. Dwight, who, at that period, was employed by him as editor of *Dwight's Journal of Music,* published by Mr. Ditson. Mr. Dwight's answer was, that he had sold his journal, but not his personal or musical opinions. He did not believe in monster jubilees: neither does any refined musician. He gave the Jubilees, both in advance and afterward, the benefit of his (let us call it mildly) disapproval. In fact, it was reported that John S. Dwight had spent the week of the first Jubilee at Nahant, where the noise of the cannon fired off to accentuate the rhythm of *God Save the Queen* (or *America,* whichever you choose to call it), and the blows on the one hundred anvils (*sic!*) in the Anvil Chorus from *Il Trovatore,* could not reach his ears and torture him.

Mr. Dwight was a tender-hearted man, and a thoroughly cultured alumnus of Harvard. He had been one of the founders and workers in the "Brook Farm" experiment, and was certainly a good sample of that band of rare souls. He has made many of the best English translations of German songs. Examine, if you will, Schubert's *Trockene Blumen,* and any of the Heine songs set to music by Robert

JOHN S. DWIGHT.

Franz or Rubinstein. His poetic and musical nature fitted him for the work. The service he has done for music is well known by every musician. With pen and voice and every effective influence, he kept alive the Harvard Symphony Concerts for quite a while against the current of indifference which was setting in.

As before said, Mr. Dwight in his musical proclivities was a very conservative man. One can honestly say he was more than that,—he was prejudiced. He was a determined fighter of the Richard Wagner cult, and, it is said, found no merit in that composer's works. His reverence for John Sebastian Bach, Beethoven, Mozart, and other old worthies does him honor; but when a man can find no grandeur in Wagner, no beauty in the *Miserere* of *Il Trovatore*, I marvel.

Every thinking musician will agree with me that J. S. Bach is the source, the fountain, the inspiration, the evangel, so to speak, of all which is great in music; that Beethoven is still " the man with the all-conquering ideas," the king; and that Mozart with his lovely melodies, his astounding contrapuntal skill, his great, passionate, dramatic instincts, may perhaps in those qualities never be excelled; still, thank God, the Giver of all good things, the end is not yet! And when there comes a man like Wagner, who enlists a large army of earnest disciples, it is almost incomprehensible that, among the best musicians and writers, there can be found many who are exactly of the J. S. Dwight way of thinking.

CHAPTER XV

IN early days our Club held a few Mendelssohn birthday festivals. The first one, February 3, 1851, given in the Melodeon, was a great success. We invited as guests all our concert subscribers, decorated the hall tastefully, and covered the face of the balcony with white cotton cloth fringed with evergreen, on which, in letters nearly a yard long, was the legend:

"Born, Feb. 3, 1809. Died in 1847."

The stage was of course the focus of our efforts. We had borrowed a plaster bust of Mendelssohn, placed it on a pedestal festooned with flowers, and put it at the front-centre of the stage. Our five music-stands were also decorated with flowers. Then we gathered together and played round this representative, so to speak, patronymic saint. He was our idol; we offered him our adoration and homage. We were young, and certainly sincere. Satisfied it was a proper thing to do, we did it, and had no *mauvaise honte*.

Nothing of that nature could be done in this

age. It would be called childish—ridiculous perhaps. People are matured, *blasé*; they will run no risk of being considered *ingénue*. We can no longer burn enthusiastic incense to any earthly idol.

At this first festival an epilogue was composed and read by a Danish gentlemen, at that time living in Lowell. I give the concluding lines:

" Great Harmonist ! Oh let the spirit wake
  Once more to higher strains thy sacred harp ;
  Methinks I feel the sacred impulse—hark !
  I hear seraphic sounds : what notes divine
  Breathe through the ravished air ! My rapt ear feels
  The harmony of heaven. Hail sacred choir !
  Immortal spirits, hail ! O Mendelssohn !
  Be this thy praise : to lead the polished mind
  To virtue's noblest heights ; to light the flame
  Of German freedom, rouse the generous thoughts,
  Refine the passions, and exalt the soul
  To love, to heaven, to harmony, and thee."

Mr. John S. Dwight, the then accomplished editor and critic of the *Commonwealth*, gives the following account of the affair :

"THE MENDELSSOHN COMMEMORATION

" The musical event of the season, at least so far as sentiment, artistic unity, and completeness, selectness, and novelty may be regarded, came off, in a way that more than realized expectation, at the Melodeon on Monday night. It was a pure festival of art. A beautiful, sincere German enthusiasm inspired it and adorned it. The Quintette Club, prompted by the sentiment of the occasion, had sent free tickets to the three hundred or more subscribers to their chamber concerts. But almost thrice that number, at an early hour, were seated in the hall, which had been tastefully and significantly decorated. In large letters of evergreen the name 'Mendelssohn' was displayed upon the front of the gallery, over the entrance, and on either side 'Born Feb. 3, 1809,' and 'Died in 1847.' In the centre of the circle, focus of all eyes and of all thoughts,—that is, in the front of the stage, before the organ,—that spot so often occupied by vain and showy solo players who seemed to place themselves before all music,—now rose the calm, pure, classic head of the true genius of the hour, a beautiful bust of Mendelssohn, crowned with laurel. We confess our thoughts were riveted to that intellectual, that unspeakably beautiful and expressive face, in whose fine and noble features one felt the union of a masculine dignity and firmness with almost a woman's feeling. And then the large, clear, exquisitely moulded dome of thought, the perfect forehead! To tell the feelings that rushed through the mind and filled it all that evening, would require more than our power of expression. It should be a poem.

"But the effect was first complete when the five young artists, with their instruments, had seated themselves around their patron saint, to interpret to us one of his quintettes. Then as the music, his own music, woke, the calm face elevated in the middle of the group seemed almost to open its eyes and move its lips; and who did not feel the music and the marble to be mutual interpreters, and that the great composer was thus doubly present to us! The sentiment of the thing was so complete that the mind involuntarily hugged the spell; and any voice of conversation, even when a strain was finished, seemed an interruption."

We duly observed many Mendelssohn birthdays, but generally in private.

It may be worth recording that we got up a Beethoven centenary birthday commemoration in Bumstead Hall. We had the best of assistance and played the entire septette, *op.* 20, with the original instruments, the piano trio, *op.* 97, in B flat (Mr. Lang at the piano),

FELIX BARTHOLDY MENDELSSOHN.

a group of songs, and a string quartette. We did our best. It was a sincere offering, and was practically the last concert the Mendelssohn Quintette Club gave in Boston on its own account.

CHAPTER XVI

IN September, 1850, Jenny Lind gave her first concert in the old Castle Garden, at the foot of Broadway, New York. Tickets were sold at five dollars each. Large amounts were also received from premiums, and there was realized from that first concert thirty-five thousand dollars—official record.

Does not the above read like exaggerated nonsense? Nevertheless, it is true history.

In 1850 there was no concert-room of decent size uptown in New York, and Mr. P. T. Barnum was allowed to alter the interior of Castle Garden in such a manner as to fit it for his purpose. It was made large enough to hold between six and seven thousand persons, the old circular form being retained.

Probably a year in advance of Jenny Lind's advent in America, Mr. Barnum began to prepare the American people to properly receive "the musical saint," "the second Santa Cæcilia," "the angel of the stage," "the most wonderful singer ever listened to by mortal ears," etc. A regular system of short paragraphs and lengthy histories was thenceforward published and copied far and near.

Lind's early history was told and re-told: the poverty; the tribulations; the childish singing-days in the streets for coppers; her singularly wonderful voice; heard by a benevolent lady; the singer "taken up" by the lady; placed in the hands of a music teacher; sent to Garcia in Paris; years of careful training; preparations for the opera; on the point of making her *début*, when,—presto! she loses her voice! Then for two long years her life was one of sadness, patience, resignation, consolation, till her voice returned, better than ever. The two years had been utilized in absorbing musical knowledge. Preparations were once more made for the public *début*. The *début* was a great success. Paris was carried by storm. Henceforward she was in demand in all the great capitals. Musical Europe lay at her feet. London went wild over her. It was discovered that she was splendid in oratorio (there was a master-stroke). I cannot say how long her operatic career lasted, but I think it was about six years.

Then she began to be serious-minded; that period was doubtless during, and by reason of, the fortuitous environment of the Exeter Hall devotees. Meantime, it was learned she was giving her wealth away to poor people, and so legitimately earning her right to be considered a saint. She could not mingle with theatre folk any more, and she renounced the opera at the period when her ability and her fame were at their zenith.

There are certain threads in this tabulated and fabulated history which were facts. Jenny Lind did give up singing in opera, and London was "in sackcloth and ashes." Deputations, remonstrants from the most aristocratic ranks, even royalty itself, pleaded for her return to the opera, but in vain.

It is believed, and doubtless it may be true, that there was a time when the powers of good and evil were wrestling for her, and it was thought that she was wavering in her new view of life's duties; in common parlance, that she was "still on the fence." In that period of doubt the opera managers redoubled their efforts, pathetically picturing the financial distress into which she had plunged them by withdrawing from the opera at a critical moment; and that so touched her soft heart that she was on the point of yielding. But when the Exeter Hall people heard of this weakening, they quadrupled their attentions, and finally won her over for good.

All these details in the newspaper histories had in them a share both of truth and nonsense. Whether true or false, every point was a good theme for a sermon or a story, and they were all adroitly, artistically, diplomatically written up by skilful romancers in the pay of the long-sighted manager, Mr. Phineas T. Barnum. The result was that the public was made to believe that saints and angels were nowhere in comparison with Jenny Lind, and that a hearing of her singing of *I Know that my Redeemer Liveth* was quite evangelizing in its effect.

She *did* sing it grandly, and with a fervor which satisfied every musician. Handel himself would have gone down on his knees to thank her for a true, devotional, musician-like performance of that fine song.

Let us now consider for a moment what the American people were at the period of Lind's visit. They were at least not *blasé;* they did not spend their summers in Europe, consequently everybody from the old world was looked upon as a trifle superior. The generality of people were of a good, church-going kind, and were (we do not say it in any depreciating spirit) rather gullible, especially when the appeals were in the line of their faith; they were therefore in that state which delights the managerial heart, that is, ready to swallow every statement put forth.

After a year of Barnum's industrious preparation, the American people were brought up to the point of giving very high prices and big premiums. A greater excitement about Jenny Lind and a stronger desire to see and hear her, were aroused than have been manufactured in regard to any other mortal man or woman, from that time to this, in any land on which the sun shines. Old people could tell you of sacrifices made to get money to hear her which would lead you to think they were all demented. And this craze was not confined to the seaboard cities. The newspaper notices had been copied inland, and people would travel long distances to hear Jenny Lind if she was not to come near them.

An Ohio friend related his experience to me. Jenny Lind was to sing in Wheeling, West Virginia, and he lived just sixty miles west, towards Columbus. He was then a boy of eighteen, and had been for three years apprenticed to a clock-maker. His father was a clergyman, with a large family and small sal-

ANTON HEKKING. *Page* 156

ary, and though a warm-hearted music lover, was too poor to think of going to hear Jenny Lind. Father and son had read together a long notice of the approaching song-festival in Wheeling, and the father had remarked with a sigh of resignation, " I wish I could hear her."

The son determined to try and go to Wheeling for that purpose. He knew it was useless to ask his father for money or permission, but he would "get there all the same." So he started off one morning with a little kit of clock-tools in his pocket, but not daring to say anything to his family. He walked till noon in the direction of Wheeling, then went into a farmhouse, and asked if they did not want their clock repaired. They "just did"; the old clock had not run for two years. The expert boy put it in running order, and the old farmer was so pleased that he gave him a Mexican silver dollar and a good dinner.

In short, my friend spent three days on the road to Wheeling, mending clocks by the way and getting a little money for each. He reached Wheeling, paid three dollars for his concert ticket, heard Jenny Lind, and returned home in a two days' march. His father asked him where he had been, and he answered that he had walked to Wheeling, mended clocks, earned money to hear Jenny Lind, and was happy. The father saw that he had a son who was made out of good stuff, embraced him, and said not one word of reproof.

I had a personal experience which will stand as evidence of the high price of tickets. When Jenny Lind came to Boston the excitement was at high-water mark. The concerts were given in the old Tremont Temple, which would hold about twelve hundred persons. I was playing in the orchestra, and doubtless wrote very rapturous letters to a certain friend describing the greatness of her singing.

One Saturday afternoon I received a telegram from my friend, who lived about forty miles from Boston, requesting me to purchase three seats for that evening's concert and meet him at the train. The party would be composed of father, mother, and daughter. There is no harm in saying now that I entertained a youthful transient passion for the latter. Were it not so there would be no story to tell.

I quickly ascertained that in order to buy three good seats I must have forty-five dollars—and to a dead certainty I did not have five dollars to my name. It was a most embarrassing position for a young "pretender." I must not show my poverty, or my chances would be slim. I had few acquaintances save among my own impecunious kind. Fortunately I was inspired to apply to Mr. John Bigelow, the good father of the Mendelssohn Quintette Club. I went to his store, then on Washington Street, opposite the head of Water Street, and laid the telegram on his desk. It was from a mutual friend, and Mr. B. looked at me smilingly; then he read it perhaps twice, and a great light broke on him. Taking in the situation he said, "Well Tommy, I suppose you have no money"; to which I answered with a lightening heart, "No, sir." He then turned to his brother Alanson, and told him to give Mr. Ryan forty-five dollars. I bought the tickets and met the friends.

Most people think that the selling at auction of the first choice of seats is a modern idea. It is not so by any means; for most distinctly there was an auction sale for Jenny Lind's first concert in Tremont Temple, Boston. The first choice of seats was run up to $640 and was bid off by Ossian E. Dodge, a comic singer who used to travel round the country giving concerts "all sole alone," accompanying himself on a guitar. Mr. Dodge shrewdly bought his ticket for a business purpose. When the Lind concert was held, it is questionable which one of the two artists, Jenny Lind or Ossian E. Dodge, was the most stared at.

Mr. Dodge's object very soon declared itself; for well-made lithographs of him could be seen in many of the shop windows, in which he was posed as singing, guitar in hand, with the legend in big type underneath, "Ossian E. Dodge, the man who gave $640 for the first choice of seats to hear the great diva, Jenny Lind." And shortly another lithograph appeared, which represented Jenny Lind in the act of being introduced by P. T. Barnum to Ossian E. Dodge, the great comic singer. I think that will pass for a sample of pretty skilful advertising. Those old worthies could give points to us moderns; for we can scarcely show anything so fine in its line.

To return to the musical part of the Lind visit to America, Mr. Barnum had engaged several good artists who were in keeping with his star. Jules Benedict, the conductor, was a composer of operas, a middle-aged man, of very fatherly aspect, and just the dignified person required to hand Jenny Lind on and

WULF FRIES.

off the stage. He was of fairly good musical reputation and an experienced man in all musical routine. Signor Salvi was one of the best tenor singers living; Signor Belletti was a very fine baritone; and Otto Goldschmidt was a brilliant pianist, who was afterward married to Jenny Lind. There was always a grand orchestra.

Jenny Lind's repertoire during her American tour was the "Casta Diva," from *Norma;* "With Verdure Clad" and "On Mighty Pens," from the *Creation;* a cavatina from *Beatrice de Tenda,* by Bellini; the great song with two flutes from the *Star of the North,* by Meyerbeer; and "Non mi Dír," from *Don Giovanni,* by Mozart. She also sang in the trio from *Il Barbier,* and, with Belletti, the duo from *L'Elisire d'Amore,* and a great variety of the Swedish folk-songs. With the latter she nearly always ended her concerts.

She used to introduce imitations of mountain echoes in the Swedish songs, and people said she did it ventriloquially, but I have always maintained that it was done by very refined *pianissimo* singing.

I have often been asked, "How much of a singer was Jenny Lind?" I can say she deserved all that was claimed for her, unmusical, nonsensical stories excepted. Her voice was of extensive range, reaching easily to D in alt,—a voice of veiled quality with something of the essence of a tear in it. She had almost unlimited execution, sang with great earnestness, and did everything in a highly finished, broad style. Such pieces as the "Casta Diva" and *I Know that my Redeemer Liveth* she sang with so devotional a sentiment that she really seemed like some inspired priestess proclaiming her faith.

Doubtless many people in Boston will remember that once when she had reached the end of the last-named song and made her bow to the audience, Daniel Webster, who was a listener, arose from his seat in the audience, and with great dignity returned her bow.

Her intonation was perfect. Benedict had written for her a very long *cadenza* to fit the end of a cavatina from *Beatrice de Tenda*. The *cadenza* was sung without accompaniment; it covered two pages of music paper, and was written in a style suited to an instrumental concerto. Towards the end there was a sequence of ascending and descending *arpeggios* of diminished sevenths which flowed into a scale of trills from a low note to one of her highest; then dwelling very long on that note and trilling on it, she gradually, tranquilly returned to the theme of the cavatina, when it was perceived that her wonderfully fine musical ear had unerringly guided her through the mazes of the long *cadenza* and brought her to the tonic note of the piece with surprising correctness of intonation.

I think she was not overrated when called a " great singer."

The desire to hear Jenny Lind led almost to a riot at her final concert in Boston. After having squeezed out of the people all the money possible at high prices, the astute P. T. Barnum hired the upper part of the just finished Fitchburg Depot. About one third of this upper floor (which was only one story up from the street) was utilized for the railroad company's offices, and they were on either side of the building, with a wide passage way in the middle which led to the hall. The offices were made simply by window sashes from floor to ceiling. In the body of the prepared concert room there were reserved seats for about fifteen hundred, and standing-room in the passage way and round the ends of seats for about three hundred more. Rumor asserted that five hundred, or even one thousand, of such " standees" were sold. That may not be true, or it may not have been by connivance of Mr. Barnum.

The concert was given in the early summer season, warm weather prevailing. Thousands of persons had perched upon the roofs of adjoining buildings and coal-sheds, and the streets round the depot were densely packed. The only means of reaching the concert room were the two corkscrew stairways at the front corners of the building. The reserved seat ticket-holders were allowed to go up into the hall first. Then at a given signal the dollar stand-ees were admitted. There was one grand rush and the unreserved space was filled in the twinkling of an eye. People packed themselves very close, and yet there was continually a cry of "Move up in front!" with an awful pressure from behind by those who were trying to get in somehow, having paid for the expected privilege.

The time came to begin the concert. The orchestra played the overture, of which probably not a note was heard. Then came Signor Belletti. His song was simply pantomime and "dumb show." Next came Jenny Lind. It was not her turn to sing, according to the programme, but Benedict brought her on to the stage, thinking her appearance would still the

JENNY LIND.

storm. It had a partial effect. She sang "On Mighty Pens," from the *Creation*. Towards the end of the piece, the people who were penned in the passageway between the offices, began to suffer from heat and lack of air. They smashed the glass partitions, and climbed in and opened the windows. The fracas and noise of breaking glass was frightful. A large number of ladies fainted; they were brought into the orchestra anteroom, and very soon overflowed into Jenny Lind's room, so great was the confusion.

An effort was made to go on with the programme, but, to the best of my recollection, there was not another note heard after Jenny Lind's song. People began to get out as best they could. It was a slow process. I know that we of the orchestra and the singers got out by corkscrew stairs at the stage end, the steps of which were all covered with mortar, laths, and pieces of joist. Providentially, the door at the foot of the stairs was unlocked, and we reached the street safely, with our instruments.

According to report, a dense mob rushed to the Revere House, where it was said Barnum stopped, but P. T., being warned of the coming storm (also according to popular history), took a hack out to Brighton and boarded a night train for New York.

It was currently reported that from three hundred to five hundred people who held dollar admissions had not been able to even reach the corkscrew-staircase entrance. I do not know whether these ticket-holders ever recovered their money.

Some little time after the above historic occurrence, Jenny Lind was married to Otto Goldschmidt, the pianist, in Boston; and the pair went to Round Hill in Northampton, Mass., where they spent their honeymoon.

Our Quintette Club had an engagement to perform the Class Day music at Amherst College. By invitation of Jenny Lind and her husband we went to Northampton a day in advance and spent it with them. We certainly had a most gracious reception and enjoyed much music together. Jenny Lind sang all kinds of songs for us, with her husband at the piano. Goldschmidt had just composed a concerto, and we tried it over with him as far as a quintette accompaniment would reach; it was its first performance. The day and evening were enjoyable. The following morning we again met and had a little more music, till the hour came when we were forced to say our farewells.

We started in a hack for Amherst, eight miles distant, in a pouring rain, which quickly made the deepest kind of mud on the alluvial plain that lies between Amherst and Northampton. Our music trunk was tied on the rear rack of the vehicle, and when we were about half-way on our journey, the entire frame broke down, and the trunk fell into the mud. The driver jumped off, rushed to a farmhouse, got a rope, bound up the contrivance, and we started again. We arrived a trifle late for our work, but we were all young, and such mishaps sit lightly on young minds. Moreover we were too full of Jenny Lind and music to be depressed by any cares of business.

CHAPTER XVII

IT may have been two years after Jenny Lind came to America that we had a visit from Catherine Hays, or Kate Hays, as she was familiarly called. Her company had Mr. Lavenu, a song writer, for conductor. I cannot now say who was the enterprising manager. The Barnum tactics were imitated, but it was not possible to get people again up to such fever heat.

Miss Hays was a good singer, and her company was comprised of good artists, among whom was a fine tenor, a son of old John Braham, of "sea songs" fame. The party made no financial success.

In 1853, Madame Sontag came to Boston with a brilliant company, Carl Eckert being the conductor. Madame Sontag, at the time of her visit, was a handsome middle-aged woman, reported to have been a startling beauty in her best, younger days, when it was said several duels, with fatal terminations, had been fought on her account.

This may have been but managerial manufactured romance. Most managers seem to think that the adroit use of such stuff is absolutely needful to create interest. Perhaps they are right, from their standpoint. But it is discouraging to conscientious performers to know that they are considered of small account if they are simply good artists whom cruel fate has tempted to remain good, honest citizens, and who have never prowled on society or "raised Cain" in any shape.

When the Sontag party first arrived in America they had with them the fine boy violinist, Paul Jullien. I think he was about fifteen years of age at that time. He played mainly Alard and Leonard pieces, and played them very brilliantly. When the company had made a limited concert tour, attended with indifferent success, it was reorganized into an operatic enterprise and the boy violinist returned to Europe. I think his career was closed by death.

I remember distinctly Sontag in her best *rôle*, "La Fille du Régiment." She was a most attractive picture in her *vivandière* costume, with the drum hanging from her neck by a "sling," and as she was a good drummer she won enormous success. She was certainly a fine actress and an excellent singer.

Carl Eckert, the conductor, is mainly remembered and known by our younger generation of singers as the composer of the *Swiss Echo Song*, written expressly for Madame Sontag.

Madame Alboni was the next very fine singer who visited America. Oh, what a glorious contralto voice was hers! It was of a silk-velvet quality (if I may be allowed to use such a figure of speech), with deeply sympathetic, expressive tones resembling very markedly the lovely reedy tones of a violoncello. Moreover, what technical wonders Alboni could accomplish with that voice! Her coloratures in songs like *Una Voce* created the same effect as a *Carnaval de Venise* performance on the violin.

Alboni's position in the European musical world was high. Her personal temperament was of the genial, *bonhomie* quality. She seemed always to be in a most happy humor, as if specially made to create joy around her. It was of her that Berlioz, who doubtless was a cruel critic in his imperative art-demands, said that what she needed to make her one of the greatest singers that ever lived, was to have a husband who would beat her daily and make her utterly wretched. She would then be able to infuse into special *rôles*, with fine effect, some of the sorrow so salutarily beaten into her by the suppositious brute of a husband.

But, Hector, just stop a minute and think it over. How could you wish that such a glorious creature as Alboni might pass through an experience like that, merely to make a more artistic " Parisian holiday ! " Perish the thought ! There are enough sad-eyed women in the world to satisfy the majority of men. Relent, Hector, relent; let happy natures remain happy, to diffuse the warmth and light of sunshine about them. Rather let us get along without sad music and turned-down lights.

CHAPTER XVIII

IN May, 1854, I was married. In the autumn we began housekeeping in Dix Place, near Eliot Street, Boston. We had certain neighbors who became our lifelong friends. I single out for brief mention one family, by reason of the great public interest then and now attending the different members thereof.

Our home was directly opposite the house in which lived Mr. and Mrs. William Lloyd Garrison with their four sons and one daughter, and certainly it was one of the interesting happenings of my life that for two years we could enjoy friendly intercourse with the famous abolitionist,—the "hounded man," the man who, perhaps, next to John Brown, had most truly acted up to the spirit of his convictions. He had even then a growing army of adorers, and certainly a very large one of haters. What he suffered at the hands of those haters is too well known to need any chronicle here. I only know that Mr. Garrison was for me a political idol; but I choose to

WILLIAM LLOYD GARRISON.

speak now simply of his charming personality in his social and domestic relations.

In his family he was the beau-ideal of a loving husband and father. It was peculiar and delightful to see him enter his house, hang up his coat and hat, and proceed as if he were a newly arrived lover. Whatever amount of friction he may have encountered in the outer world, it was at once forgotten. His demeanor to the members of his family revealed a most sweet and loving disposition.

Mrs. Garrison was a good reflection of her husband's character. Indeed I used to think she was a kind of saint, because she was like a good mother in our family when our first daughter was born. I gave piano lessons to their little girl, Fanny, who in time became the wife of Mr. Henry Villard. The sons of Mr. Garrison have given a good account of themselves. The third son, Wendell Phillips Garrison, has been for many years the editor of *The Nation*.

Naturally, I had the opportunity to become acquainted with many of the rank and file of (in the common parlance of that day) "those d——d abolitionists" who acknowledged Mr. Garrison as master. All these people were really of a peculiar type, most thoroughly unselfish, idealists,—"cranks," if you please; otherwise, people with a religion which set them to working for the good of others.

It was also in the natural order of things that if I knew Mr. Garrison I should know Theodore Parker. I regard it as a piece of great good fortune to have been in the world at that period, and to have heard that fearless preacher. Those were the times before the Civil War, when clergymen and others were often mobbed because they revealed the iniquity of human slavery. Parker and Wendell Phillips, when they preached or lectured, often required a body-guard to escort them from their homes to the Boston Music Hall and back. It seems almost an incredible story, but it is true history, well known in Boston.

Closely allied, in one sense, with all those good souls, was the well beloved Rev. Thomas Starr King, pastor of the Hollis Street Church. What a bright man he was, and how animating in his pulpit utterances!

He was passionately fond of music. I remember that when Mr. J. Trenkle was organist of the church, it was part of the musical programme that after the second hymn the organist should make an extensive improvisation or play some set piece of fine music. Mr. King believed it was as worthy a jubilate as any human speech could utter ; and that good music, artistically given, attuned his moral and mental faculties to a fine spiritual state, and invigorated him for the sermon yet to be delivered. It is clear that he was inspired in that belief, and many years ahead of a large share of the human family.

We must not overlook one historical fact : that Rev. Thomas Starr King was unofficially sent out to California to keep that State in the Union. He succeeded in his undertaking, as has been recorded by better pens than mine. I simply wish to express my joy in having known him, and having been for a while under his fascinating influence.

I recall with great pleasure the time when I had the honor of working in collaboration with Dr. Oliver Wendell Holmes, in an attempt to make a national hymn. A short time after President Lincoln's call for troops, Dr. Holmes did me the honor of coming to see me at my rooms in the Pavilion on Tremont Street. After mutual greetings, the Doctor said that his friend, Mr. William Schultze (our Quintette Club first violin), under whose able tuition he was studying the violin, had told him that Mr.

Ryan was just the man to make, in conjunction with him, a hymn acceptable to the people.

It is to be remembered that the Civil War had just begun, and calls were made through the newspapers for a national song; it was said that we could no more dispense with it than we could with a flag. A group of patriots in New York City had offered a prize for such a hymn. Dr. Holmes thought we ought to try for the prize. I was eager to do my share. To collaborate with such a man was an honor and a personal delight.

Our *modus operandi* was first to select a strongly marked march-rhythm, then he was to write a few verses to fit it, and when that was satisfactorily done I was to write an original melody to his words. The plan was good and practical. For the rhythm I selected *Washington's March.* Then Dr. Holmes began work.

He was a "chain-lightning" poet in his rapid invention of verses. Furnished with pencil and paper, he sat at the table and I sang with a good lusty voice the melody of the march; singing it alternately slow or quick, soft or loud. After a few trials, he "caught on" to the rhythm and quickly found the cor-

MRS. WILLIAM LLOYD GARRISON.   *Page 149*

responding poetical measure. From that moment he went on making verses; and the rapidity with which he changed words, ideas, and poetic figures, transposed lines, dropped certain trains of ideas and brought out stronger ones, was extraordinary to me. The verses grew under his fingers as rapidly as one might write an ordinary epistle,—the Doctor singing or humming the melody, or beating the rhythm on the table.

We spent perhaps an hour in these researches or exercises till the Doctor had covered perhaps two pages of foolscap with his rough drafts. He then left me, taking them with him, and in a few days he brought me a pencilled copy (which I have kept) of the first verse and chorus that he had finally "whipped into shape," and which, he said, satisfied his judgment. Later on, he brought the entire hymn written with ink (which I now have), five verses in all, entitled *Union and Liberty*. Under that caption, the hymn was printed later, and afterward included in a collection of his poems.

I give the first verse only:

"UNION AND LIBERTY.

"Flag of the heroes who left us their glory,
  Borne through their battle-fields' thunder and flame,

Blazoned in song and illumined in story,
Wave o'er us all who inherit their fame !
    Up with our banner bright,
    Sprinkled with starry night,
Spread its fair emblems from mountain to shore ;
    While through the sounding sky
    Loud rings the nation's cry,—
Union and Liberty, one evermore ! "

We then tried to make another set of verses of a less strongly marked martial rhythm. I quite forget the melody they were to fit, but it was to be rather slow, like the Austrian Hymn.

The poet made six verses and a chorus, entitled *Freedom, our Queen*, beginning with,

" Land where the banners wave last in the sun."

This set of verses is also published among his poems.

We sent on our attempts to New York, as doubtless many other people did, but nothing ever came of it. No answer was returned, no examination made, no prize awarded, so far as we could learn. We had our pleasant labor for our pains. But I prize the memory of having collaborated with one of America's greatest poets.

CHAPTER XIX

DOUBTLESS it will be of interest to some of our old friends to have the various changes in the membership of the Mendelssohn Quintette Club indicated. The first to retire was Edward Lehman (flute). He was succeeded by Gustav Krebs. The next was Francis Riha (violin), succeeded by Carl Meisel. This latter was an honored member for about twenty years. He was a fine violinist, a man of charming personal character, and is still alive, working in his profession in Southern California.

About the tenth year, August Fries retired on account of ill health, and was suceeeded by William Schultze, the former concert-master of the Germania Musical Society. Schultze remained our first violin for about twenty years. During this period Mr. Wulf Fries, 'cellist, retired after an honorable service with the Club of twenty-three years. Mr. Fries is still an active worker, and lives in Roxbury. He was succeeded by Rudolph Hennig, who remained for about eight years, and was replaced by Fritz Giese for five years. Then there were a few temporary changes of 'cellists till Anton Hekking came. It is to be seen that the Club has had, from first to last, the best of 'cellists to help make its reputation.

When Meisel retired, he was succeeded for four years by the excellent violinist, Carl Hamm. Then came Gustav Dannreuther, well known in the musical world, who is now in New York City, at the head of a quartette club bearing his name. He was succeeded by the well-known and popular violinist, C. W. Allen, Thiele, and others.

During the period of these changes, various good flautists, such as Beyer and Goering, were with us. Next came the brilliant flautist, Edward Heindl, who played with us for twelve or thirteen years, and was replaced by Schade (latterly with the Boston Symphony), who was followed by Henneberg, and Rodenberg up to date.

When we lost our first violin, Schultze, we lost one of the most genial men with whom I ever came in contact. He was not only a fine violinist, but an excellent general musician, a devoted student of literature, quite a linguist, an inexhaustible story-teller, a generous-hearted man, and always a gentleman in the fullest sense of the word.

Schultze left us to accept a professorship in the Wesleyan University at Syracuse, N. Y., but after a few years of service he had a paralytic stroke, from which he only partly recovered, though he managed to work a few years longer. One morning in 1890, while playing the violin at a recital, his vital forces suddenly gave out and he almost fell to the floor. His friends came to his assistance, but the good spirit which had been such a source of pleasure to them had quitted its earthly tenement. He died just as a good man would wish to die, in harness and surrounded by his pupils.

Mr. S. Jacobsohn replaced Schultze for two seasons. He was a splendid violinist, a grand player in quartette. He could play with a tender sentiment quite surpassing all players I have ever heard, without exception; and when fully aroused he became a passionate player. Altogether he was a master artist.

The Club, so far as good playing goes, reached "high-water mark" with Jacobsohn as first violin. The members at that time were: S. Jacobsohn, Gustav Dannreuther, Thomas Ryan, Edward Heindl, Rudolph Hennig. We had in addition the contrabassist, Alexander Heindl, for two years; also Mr. Manoly for the same length of time, both gentlemen being virtuosi on the contrabass. At the end of these four years we came to the conclusion that we were simply giving ourselves a musical gratification; the public at large never appreciated the increase of tone, so for financial reasons we gave up the contrabass.

Mr. Bernard Listemann, the brilliant violinist, replaced Jacobsohn for one season. Then came Edward Heimendahl for two seasons, an excellent man and violinist, with marked ability as a composer. He was succeeded by the remarkably fine violinist, Mr. Isidor Schnitzler, at present one of the first violins and soloist of the Boston Symphony.

One episode in the Club's history may be of some little interest. We arrived one morning in a certain Michigan town, and were met at the railroad station by a friend of long standing. In a very serious tone of voice he informed me that another good friend of the Club, a 'cello amateur, was so far gone in consumption that his physician and family had given him up; he would probably die during the day. The expected visit of the Mendelssohn Quintette Club had apparently kept him alive; he wanted to hear the *Tema con Variazioni* from

RUDOLPH HENNIG.

the Schubert D-minor Quartette before he gave up the ghost. He had placed a sum of money in the teacher's hands to pay us. Would we gratify him?

The situation quite shocked me. I said, "Of course we will play, but don't talk of money."

The sick friend was at the same hotel in which we were to be quartered. The plan was for us to play in a room at some little distance from his, but with both doors open. He wanted the music to reach his ears as a last sweet echo of his departing musical pleasures.

We prepared to play very soon after our arrival at the hotel. To me, who knew the young man well, it was a very solemn moment. To play under such circumstances required some self-possession.

On a lower floor in the hotel lay a brother of the sick man who was also in a rapid decline, and very near death. The mother was in attendance at his bedside. Scarcely had we reached the middle of the piece, when a messenger from the mother came to request us to stop, for the brother down-stairs was so affected that she feared immediate death. We ceased playing. This latter brother died during the ensuing night; but the one who wanted the music lived on, and some favorable change occurred which gave him a fresh lease of life,—good for some years after the time he thought he was to hear his parting *Swan Song*.

This unique masterwork of Franz Schubert has always been the one oftenest asked for, and I must mention one other solemn occasion when we had to play it. A young lady died in Dorchester who had been one of our earnest friends and music lovers. She left a sum of money with her brother in order that he might engage the Quintette Club to play certain selections at her funeral. She had planned the entire function. We played in a room adjoining the parlor where the religious service was held. We began with the *Swan Song*, playing it with muted strings. That was followed by prayer. Then we played one of the *Seven Last Words of Christ*,—music composed for string quartette. Next the burial service was read, followed by addresses from friends; and we ended the exercises by playing another of the *Seven Last Words*.

This was certainly an occasion when firmness and composure were needed. Imagine having to play music of such technical difficulty at such a time, in such a situation, where the burden of the song, "Death and the

Maiden," had its counterpart in the adjoining chamber, for there was death, and there also was the maiden.

I knew that the girl during the brief span of her life had a very elevated and spiritual love for music; it spoke to her as nothing else did. And her brother told me she was steadfast in the belief that she would be present in spirit during these last earthly rites, and would again hear the music she loved so well.

Knowing these facts, I was greatly affected while playing. They kept surging through my thoughts and brought me to the very verge of sobbing. When we first began, I must say, in familiar language, it was "just awful." I shall never forget it, and hope never to pass through a similar experience.

CHAPTER XX

IN the year 1859, the Quintette Club made its first concert trip to Philadelphia, Baltimore, and Washington, accompanied by Mrs. J. H. Long, a fine soprano, of Boston. The trip was successful, and we made an impression which encouraged us to repeat the venture many times. This little concert *tournée* was practically our first playing outside of New England. It seemed to us a very grand thing to give publicly advertised concerts in those large cities, and to attract good audiences. All was new and interesting.

One experience is worth relating. I had a letter of introduction to Mr. X., a great man of the period, the publisher and editor of the principal Washington newspaper. Calling to see him on the day of the first of our two concerts in the old Willard Hall, I was courteously received, and after I had explained the motive of my call, I expressed the hope that he would send a reporter to the concert that evening so as to have a detailed report in the next morning's paper, and thus help us to a full house on the second night. The good old gentleman replied that his daughter was the only person whom he could trust to write musical notices for his paper. She was not in very good health, but if she could not attend the concert he would have something written up for the morning's issue without fail.

The concert attracted a fair attendance, and gave evident pleasure. In next morning's paper we found the "something without fail" in the shape of a glowing article; but,—*mirabile dictu!*—we were all singers instead of players!—a kind of Hutchinson-family arrangement; that being the sort of music then most enjoyed by the public.

The notice in question contained ecstatic praise of the soprano, and also of the sympathetic alto, declaring that so good a voice had never before been heard in Washington. The tenor "had the true timbre of a tenor voice,"—there was no suspicion there of a light baritone. The bass was "a really organ-like support for the beautiful musical superstructure." The concert was quite an ideal one, etc.

These are not the exact words, perhaps, but they are the substance of the notice, which I now have, filed away in my treasury of funny happenings.

It did us good service, nevertheless, and we had a full house the second night. Probably if we had been described as a club of instrumental players, composed of "four violins and a bass "(which is the musically intelligent way in which we are often even now depicted), our fate would have been sealed in Washington. Classic music is still *caviare* to many people, and thirty-six years ago it was a thing of dull and dubious character to the uninitiated.

As years rolled on, people from the western states who had heard our club play in or around Boston, often asked, "Why don't you come out West?"

Accordingly I made practical inquiries in regard to a concert trip, and received encouraging replies. Still I thought it would not be safe to try it unless we had some "star" with us, to add to our attractions. We finally reached the venturing-point, and engaged as stars Miss Adelaide Phillips, the well-known contralto, and Camille Urso, the distinguished lady violinist. We were managed by Harry McGlennen, the well-known advertising manager, so long at the Boston Theatre, and

CAMILLE URSO.

made a short trip of three or four weeks, meeting with good success.

Madame Urso deserves something more than a mere passing mention. She is easily the most remarkable violin player who ever came to America and made her home among us. I well remember her as she appeared at her *début* in Jonas Chickering's piano rooms. She was then a little girl of eleven, with the same sad and interesting face that she has now. Yet, when not playing, she is full of fun, and her conversation is richly humorous.

Her playing as a child was very artistic. She made her *début* in the "Fantaisie" on *Il Pirate*, by Artot, accompanied by her father on the piano, and she won an immediate success.

Her career is too well known to demand any detailed account from me, but I wish to emphasize the fact that she has made constant progress in her art. She has played all the modern masterworks, the great concertos, in the principal concerts in New York, Boston, and, indeed, in all the larger cities from Maine to California, and she is still earning laurels.

She has played so often with our club, and I know her fine points so well, that it is not easy for me to speak of her playing except in unqualified eulogy.

To return to my narrative, after that trial-trip I decided that it was a safe thing to undertake a travelling concert season, and that we did not need "stars" to attract audiences. Individual star singers and players had been heard everywhere in the West; *ensemble* playing was the novelty. We prepared for the long season's travel, and engaged one of our charming home singers to accompany us, Miss Addie S. Ryan (not a daughter of mine, as many imagine). She had a rich and very sympathetic voice, was a good all-round singer, and very "taking" in ballads. She became a great favorite wherever heard.

The financial result of the long season of travel was good, and for many years we made similar trips, and (which will surprise many persons) without the help of any advance agent. All details and arrangements for our appearance in towns and cities were made by correspondence. To be sure, it kept me busy, but the West of that period was not the West of to-day. To a certain degree we had the entire western country to ourselves. There were no other musical people travelling. There were very many minstrel companies (which did not injure us), and a few dramatic troupes. We were in demand everywhere;

the main trouble was to get dates. Money was plentiful,—every one was "flush" after the war.

Before long we began to have imitators,— either in '63 or '64. The first musical organization to follow in our wake was the "Redpath Parlor Opera Company," organized in Boston. It was a quartette of good home-singers. Clara Nickels was the soprano, Flora Barry the alto, Charles Clark the tenor, Edward Payson the bass and John A. Howard the pianist. They began first as a concert company, and afterward wisely turned into a parlor opera company, doing acts of either *Martha* or *Don Pasquale*. They were very successful and in a little while they in their turn had imitators.

Little by little companies enlarged their personnel till the full-fledged affair appeared and captured the country with *Pinafore*. I gladly turn over to future historians this line of the divine art of music, knowing that they will have a "nice little job" to keep track of the numberless big and little opera companies who are now actively competing with each other in the struggle for existence.

In 1868 the Club was in Chicago. The time had come when I could no longer dispense with the services of an advance agent,—competition was becoming active. I secured a good one in Mr. D. H. Elliot, who was a Georgian by birth, and had been a Confederate officer of marked ability. I found him to be a man of wonderful managerial resources, so I let him have free rein.

He opened with a brilliant *coup*. A big political convention was being held in the Crosby Opera House. Elliot had five thousand little "dodgers" made of gossamer paper, four by six inches in size, on which was printed: " The Mendelssohn Quintette Club of Boston, the most wonderful body of instrumentalists in America, will soon arrive in Chicago, and will play for one week in the Crosby Opera House. Tell your friends the joyful news." At a given moment during the convention, these five thousand little bits of paper (like Chinese printed prayers) came fluttering down from the cupola of the opera house to all parts of the assembly. Everybody grabbed for them, and a point was gained. The daily papers exploited the joke, and excited enough interest to give us six good houses for one week. We paid two hundred dollars per night for the opera house. That fact now reads like a fairy tale. Those were great times after the war ; everybody had money and spent it right royally.

I must relate another exploit of our brave ex-Confederate soldier. We had made a little summer concert trip to Niagara Falls, and gave one or two concerts. It is to be remembered that immediately after crossing the bridge over the rapids to Goat Island, there used to be a small paper mill on the right-hand side, the walls of which were built directly on the edge of the wild, rushing waters. Elliot often did the unexpected thing. This time he went into the office of the paper mill, and asked if they had any objection to his putting up a poster for a concert on the walls of the mill over the rapids. They laughed derisively and said they had no objection,—" Go ahead."

We were using as advertising material at that time, a long, showy streamer—each letter a full sheet—which bore in black letters shaded by red on a white ground, " Mendelssohn Quintette Club of Boston." It was a stunning thing ; it could be read five miles distant.

Elliot borrowed a skiff, put all his pasting and other materials into it, hired some good, reliable men to assist, and got the skiff across the bridge and into the water. He then boarded it, with one man to help, and his other assistants on shore paid out a long rope, to which the boat was attached, until it reached the wall, on which he pasted up every letter and returned to *terra firma* in safety. It was a crazy, dangerous thing to do, but it paid. Everybody went to see the poster, which could be read easily at the old Grand Trunk Railway bridge, two miles distant, and all along the Canada shore. The desired point was gained; it excited all kinds of remarks, and I believe remained upon the wall for two years. The paper and paste were good, and no one cared or dared to risk getting it down.

Another story characteristic of Elliot is worth telling. At Geneva, N. Y., a minstrel troupe had just preceded us. Their pictorial bills were still up, depicting the minstrels in full artistic action on the stage. The local bill-poster, infatuated, doubtless, with "them lovely pictures," and hating to cover them up, as they were so æsthetically ornamental to the town, conceived the idea of pasting our big streamers directly above them, and our three-sheet bills on each side, thus making an exact frame for their picture. To all appearance, the whole thing was one show,—the Mendelssohn Quintette Club were the minstrels, or the minstrels were the Mendelssohn Quintette Club, just as the casual passer-by might infer.

D. H. ELLIOT.

Elliot was so pleased with the completeness of the unwonted combination, that he borrowed from the poster-man his working clothes, dressed up in them, got the paste-bucket, brush, and ladder, took up a position at the side of the picture, pointed to it with evident admiration, and had a photographer take a shot at the whole, and thus made it immortal.

Mr. Elliot was a good, level-headed American. After travelling for us two years he determined to settle down and begin work for a permanent home. He has been for some years in Florida, and is one of Mr. Plant's right-hand men, which, as may be known, means very much. Morever, the State of Florida sent him to the Paris, Vienna, and Columbian Expositions, to show up its resources.

Our old agent still often travels long distances to see and hear us; then we have a good, square chat and, like old soldiers, we go over the skirmish-lines and battle-fields once more.

CHAPTER XXI

IN 1872, as our Club, individually and collectively, were tired of travelling and of being away so much from our families, we determined to try to establish ourselves again in Boston. With ample preparation and all the thought we were capable of concentrating on the work, we three men, Mr. Schultze, Mr. Heindl, and myself, began the venture of establishing the " National College of Music."

We had a faculty of genuine artists, comprising: Vincenzo Corillo from the Royal Music School in Naples, principal vocal teacher; Mr. Charles Hayden, assistant; and Mr. B. J. Lang, head of the piano department. The assistant piano teachers were all brilliant young men whom Lang had taught and developed, namely: Mr. Geo. W. Sumner, well known and beloved as organist for seventeen years at the Arlington Street Church, Mr. Hiram Tucker, Mr. W. F. Apthorp, Mr. Dixie, and Mr. J. Q. Adams. All these men would naturally teach according to the Lang method, and that certainly was a commendable system. As teachers of string instruments, we had of course the Quintette Club.

We held a matinée of classic music every Saturday, and the pupils were expected to be present. Those who were capable of playing *ensemble* music had therefore frequent opportunity of doing it with the Quintette Club. The same privilege was given to singers.

Our plans were all right, and we started off with goodly numbers,—not far from two hundred pupils. In October, just one month later, the great Boston fire occurred; and it made everybody poor. The majority of the pupils were from the city or neighborhood, and over one half of them were forced to notify us that they could not continue their attendance another term. The fire really killed our school. We worried along to the end of the year, met our losses as best we could, and returned to our old system of travelling,—in short, "took to the road" again.

A fearful amount of time is spent on railroad trains while jogging from town to town in our country of great distances. At first it is novel enough, with its ever-changing kaleidoscope of experiences, to make the time go quickly; but when the second or third season of such travel comes round, what a "demnition grind" it is! The very disagreeable people one sometimes meets, the waiting at junctions, the unwholesome food, the running of trains at very unseasonable hours, as far as the traveller's comfort is concerned,—all these make a sum total of petty miseries which is very considerable. In such circumstances, if some one comes along who at once shortens the hours and sweetens the life,—even to the limited extent of making one forget the worst part of it,—that person is a very welcome companion.

Just such a desirable person entered our car one dull, rainy day on the New York Central Railroad,—a very attractive lady lecturer and a marvellously fine story-teller. She employed so much verve and action in her narrations that one could almost *see* the scenes described. Knowing her well, I was delighted to meet her again and to learn that we were to be travelling companions for some hours.

Every story-teller knows there are two kinds of listeners,—the simply attentive listeners, and the encouraging, inspiring ones. On the day in question, I must have been of the latter kind, for my friend unreeled story after story, in most of which she figured as principal; and

I am sure she invented nothing, though possibly she may have added a little coloring matter. The stories are too good not to put one or two in print for future Bunsbys. For the sake of convenience I will call the lady "Miss A."

She had been engaged to lecture in a rather small town in Northern Illinois, and it was her first visit to that section of country. On account of some misunderstanding as to the hour of arrival, there was no committee-man, with welcoming face, to meet her. To a lady lecturer travelling alone, words of welcome and regretful farewells coupled with the "hope that we shall have you again next year," constitute the greater part of her reward,—omitting for the moment, if you please, the tender little check received after the work is done.

Finding no one to meet her, and knowing the name of the hotel where she was to stop, Miss A. was the first one to enter its waiting 'bus, and, taking one of the seats farthest from the door, she awaited further developments. In a few minutes two ladies entered, who eyed her wonderingly and exchanged glances and remarks in a way that was not sweetly comforting—soon interrupted, however, by the entrance of several men with musical instruments. The newcomers also looked questioningly at Miss A., but business was evidently on hand, for they began to take out their instruments from bags and cases. Miss A. also noticed that a man spread a cover of fringed white cloth over each horse, bearing some legend which she could not make out, and ornamented with designs of an artistic nature at the corners, groups of banjos, mandolins, fiddles, triangles, flutes, castanets, etc. Then the men opened the windows in the 'bus, and " the band began to play."

Just imagine the young lady lecturer shrinking into her corner, the stunning noise of ten or twelve brass instruments, reinforced by a big bass drum on the roof of the stage, every blow on which seemed to strike her on the top of her head, and also to act on the honest, staid horses like a bunch of exploding firecrackers tied to their tails. Away they flew and almost brought about the crack of doom to the 'bus and its occupants. The bandmen, however, taught by previous experiences, perceived that a fifty measures' rest would be a good thing just then, and stopped playing until the horses quieted down. After a while they began again, and as the man on top thumped *mezzo forte* this time the horses seemed only to be rejuvenated by the sweet sounds and behaved decorously.

The *cortège* went pretty much all over town, and finally halted at the hotel. The bandmen and the two ladies got out of the 'bus. Miss A., summoning up all the life that was left in her, and separating herself from the crowd, got out with all becoming dignity. The landlady, who was evidently waiting for her, came forward, received her very cordially, and conducted her to a cosy, charming room, where she fluttered and flattered with an *impressement* that only one woman can show to another.

Finally she left her, saying that tea would be ready soon, and she would meet her at the dining-room door. The poor martyr, thankful for the momentary quiet, gave vent to her pent-up anguish in a woman's usual, blessed way,—namely, tears,—bemoaning the fate which had sent her on the road to drift about among such scenes and people.

The soothing influence of quiet and rest soon restored her composure, and she descended to the dining-room. Duly met by the landlady, she was conducted to a separate table, where covers for two were laid, and it really was a "nice spread." The good hostess, who had, unasked, fastened herself on Miss A.

as a companion, chatted and buzzed and amused her greatly.

The repast over, the landlady, evidently with some unusual pleasure still in anticipation, conducted Miss A. to her room. Unable to contain herself any longer, she burst out with,—

"Now, I want to see your gowns."

"My gowns! what gowns?"

"Why, your stage gowns."

"My stage gowns! I have no other gowns than the one I have on."

"But"—in a very pleading tone—"where are your play-gowns for the stage?"

"Play-gowns! Oh, I see! there is some mistake. I don't play."

"Don't you belong to the show?"

"No, no; I'm not up in the art-world like that. I am only a humble lecturer, and am to speak in the church to-night."

This confession fairly caused the landlady to turn pale and gasp for breath. The full extent of the fraud she had practised on herself was so great that it completely robbed her of power to speak; but it brought an expression of disgust and contempt into her countenance which was more scathing than a dictionary's whole store of epithets. Turning her back on Miss A. she vanished from view, and

Page 85

did not show herself again while that lady stayed at the hotel.

The scene of another story was laid in a remote section of Wisconsin. A (very) "Young Men's Society" were to hold a series of lectures for the first time in their town, and Miss A. was to open the course. When she stepped out of the warm and comfortable car, she realized very quickly that it was a cold, wintry day, little adapted to the reception that had been planned for her. The entire society, some twenty in number, had delegated themselves to meet the lecturer, and they were drawn up in line on the sidewalk like a military company. The leader came forward, led Miss A. to the line, and ceremoniously introduced her to every Brown, Smith, Jones, etc., of them all. This duty done, he wiped his brow and looked around as if for some one to tell him what to do next. Miss A. suggested that, as it was so very cold, she would like to go to her hotel. The company escorted her to a one-horse sleigh, waiting near, the leader handed her in,—the young men watching every motion,—got in himself, and then with that true though timid gallantry characteristic of the rural young American, offered her the reins. She thanked him, but declined on the ground that he probably knew the way and the horse better than she did.

When evening came, the whole youthful regiment was on hand to escort Miss A. to the little theatre where the lecture was to be given. The house was packed. She took off her wraps and followed her leader to the stage, which was decorated with a small table, a pitcher of water, and a tumbler. There was also a long, old-fashioned settee, with legs under the middle and at either end. Taking a seat at the farther end she noticed that it tilted down with her. Presently a large, heavily built clergyman came on to the stage, sat down on the other end of the settee, and up she went, her feet no longer touching the floor. Everybody laughed. The tilting was great fun to the good-natured, honest, typical country audience.

Having nothing else to do, Miss A. scanned the assemblage. Foremost, leaning his folded arms on the edge of the stage, was a young man in a red flannel shirt (probably one of the fire company), who watched all her movements with the most careful attention, never once taking his eyes from her. Finally the reverend gentleman arose rather suddenly, letting Miss A.'s end of the settee down with a thud, which brought out another good-natured laugh from all parts of the house. The reverend gentleman began the proceedings with a long-winded introductory speech, under which infliction the audience grew more and more restless, until the young man in the red shirt, unable to hold in any longer, blurted out, "Dry up, old man, and give the young gal a chance!" Whereupon the prologue came to an end and the lecture was delivered without further incident.

Miss A. told me a third story, which reveals her good and generous, but impulsive character. She was engaged to lecture in a college town in Ohio, and was met at the station by one of the professors, at whose house she was to be entertained. On the way thither the gentleman expressed his sentiments in regard to women's rights in so offensive a way that he roused in her the strongest kind of an antipathy. He was so opinionated and arrogant that, to use her own words, "He set all my woman's blood boiling when airing his opinions." I inferred that the unlucky man had been "in for it," and had unquestionably received the punishment that she was quite competent to give.

Arriving at the house, Miss A. inquired for her hostess, and the gentleman replied that she was busy preparing supper. She had a large number of boarders—students—and was attending to her duties "as a good housewife should" (strongly emphasized); by which speech the man of course floundered deeper into Miss A's disesteem.

In due time a messenger came to Miss A.'s room to say that tea was ready and they were "waiting prayers." Miss A. replied that she would wait till the lady of the house could see her. That must have raised a breeze, for the good housewife soon came up, in breathless haste. The picture which Miss A. had mentally conjured up of the lady fitted her perfectly. She was a thin, anxious, nervous, overworked woman. After a minute's conversation the two ladies descended to prayers and tea. While at the tea-table Miss A. tried her best to draw out the lady hidden in the drudge, to help her to be properly esteemed by all present, and to have them understand that the wife was filling an honorable position at the head of the table, though she had previously prepared the food with her own hands.

In the course of the conversation Miss A. modestly expressed the hope that her hostess would be pleased with her lecture.

"Oh, dear me," was the answer, "I cannot go! I have too much to do. I have no help, and I must wash and put away the tea things, etc."

Miss A. replied that she would help her do all that,—and in fact there would be no lecture that evening if she did not go with her. Miss A. carried her point, sent for a hack, and took the lady to and from the lecture, totally ignoring Mr. Pomposity. Her lecture being on the subject of righting women's wrongs, she thought it was as well to begin righting them, or fighting for them, then and there.

I remember telling Miss A. of a certain experience of my own which is possibly worth repeating.

Calling one day on the City Attorney of a small town in Northern Illinois, and waiting in his office for a little transaction to be effected between the attorney and a caller, I noticed on the mantelpiece two well-known statuettes, one representing a "Cavalier," the other a "Roundhead," both illustrative of English history. Examining the Cavalier I saw a small inscription on its base which puzzled me. It was "General Grant." The make-up of the figure was that of a cavalier soldier, with a large felt hat and feather, an arquebus on the left shoulder, a sword at his side. The Roundhead had cropped hair, surmounted by a leather, pot-like head-covering, and his right hand grasped a long Cromwellian sword, point straight down. On the base of this figure was written, "General Butler."

Knowing the figures and their significance, I turned to the attorney and asked for the "joke." "Well," said he, with a hearty laugh, "I've had my money's worth of fun from those little things, which I bought from a travelling art dealer, little dreaming of the endless questions and explanations they would require. One day, before I affixed those generals' names, a good honest rustic asked, 'What be them, anyway?' I said, 'I suppose you have heard of the statutes of Illinois?' He said, "Yes." I said, "Well, them's 'em," and that satisfied him. Very soon I perceived that I must have some other plan to permanently switch off remark, so I attached the names. One caller very closely examined the figures, and after some cogitation he remarked, "I did n't think Grant looked like that, but Butler is just splendid; any one can see it is like him."

CHAPTER XXII

IT may be well to say that I am not undertaking to write the musical history of the United States, nor even of Boston; but I believe the Jubilees are as worthy of being put on record as would be a first performance in America of the *Parsifal* by Richard Wagner; though in comparison with the latter, the Jubilee music is like a boy compared with a man. But without the first, the other could not be. *Parsifal* is the man fully grown (some think he is the *ne plus ultra*), while the Jubilees represent the boy,—the tearing, rowdy young fellow, in his first stage of musical growth.

There are musical people of the present age who ask, "What were those Jubilees you talk about?" Some of them may add, "I find in my good mother's library a stack of chorus music marked 'The Jubilee Collection'; and among those pieces are works written by our native composers, together with great oratorios and some trash. What does it all mean? When did the Jubilees occur?"

I will try to answer those questions, premising that there could not have been Jubilees without Patrick Sarsfield Gilmore; and we must know his history to know that of the Jubilees.

It is well understood that all talented men are of Irish parentage, for that naturally includes the present writer (!) as well as Mr. Gilmore,—or rather " P. S.," as all his friends called him. As a boy he lived in Salem, Mass., and quite early in life he was a member of the Salem Band, and afterward its leader. His next step forward made him, in 1852, a member of the somewhat famous " Ordway Minstrels," in Boston, then playing in the little hall of the historical " Province House," where, in colonial times, the governors and nabobs held high court,—or "high jinks," as we may properly call it.

If we here allow a spirit of discursive moralizing to take possession of us, we shall have a fine chance to make mental pictures of the old colonial days, to see in fancy the red-coated king's officers, the bedizened governor and his courtiers, the young bucks and belles of the period, the guards of honor in and about the diminutive but cozy little place of royal revelry, and then to compare it all with an enter-

PATRICK S. GILMORE.

tainment prepared for our modern republican pleasure-loving people,—so entirely different, even in their pleasures. In old times, "pleasures" meant chiefly eating, drinking, dancing, hunting, and love-making. The latter, in its primitive essentials, remains the same, and doubtless will till the end of time, but in other things our modern system of pleasures is vastly different from that of the colonial days. It is true we eat and drink, and we dance a little, but we have evolved a large class of people to entertain us in various ways, and to do it without any effort on our part. One species of this entertainment is, or was, negro minstrelsy; perhaps we might call it "low jinks." We see a band of these fun-providing people holding their revelry in that same Province House hall, and what a cruel contrast is thus made by the irony of fate! Where English nobles once held court, we now see the Irish boy, Patrick Gilmore, snapping his fingers in derision at nobles or their king,—and yet only in the spirit of professional fun, for he with his good brethren are thus earning their daily bread.

From out the frame of that picture we may now withdraw the aspiring boy, P. S. Gilmore, for he shortly after graduated into one of the military bands in Boston. Step by step he climbed the ladder, and finally we had "Gilmore's Band." "P. S." was an active, restless "hustler," and his band was soon on the top of the wave. When the war broke out, Gilmore showed at once the stuff he was made of. He was an ardent "off-for-the-war" man. Meetings to help along enlistments for the army and navy were being held everywhere. Gilmore and his full band constantly played at these meetings, and I dare say played out of pure patriotism. With his band in gay uniforms and ribbons flying from their hats, as in old days, he even paraded the streets of Boston, drumming up recruits for the Massachusetts 24th Regiment.

The next step was that he and his whole band volunteered as soldiers, regularly enlisted as the band of the 24th, and with that regiment went to the war. It is on record that he and his men were always on hand to cheer up "the boys" with good music when they most needed it, and he even got some of the bright young spirits of that crack regiment to form a minstrel company. In fact, he showed his energy and good fellowship in every situation.

After about a year's service in North Carolina, his band, like most of the regimental bands, was mustered out. General Banks, commanding the Department of New Orleans, urged Mr. Gilmore to go to that city and become the chief director of music in his command. He accepted, and was a very popular man in that capacity. He organized one very large school-children's music festival, and it doubtless gave him a good preliminary experience in managing large numbers of performers.

When the "cruel war was over" Gilmore went back to Boston, and once more had "to hustle for a living." He reorganized his band, brought it up to its best estate, and for several seasons gave Sunday night sacred and popular concerts in Music Hall or Boston Theatre. He was a venturesome manager, paying high for drawing cards, and usually had a big orchestra and chorus in addition to his band. He did all the drilling and directing of the musical forces himself, attended to the financial details, and managed to get valuable assistance from the newspapers; in fact, he manifested an energy which was astounding. His large "pull" on the military element in Boston was a great help to him. In the midst of this activity in public entertainments, he formed a partnership (Gilmore & Wright) for the manufacture of band instruments.

I mention all these points to show that Mr. Gilmore was a very bright, energetic man. And whether he lost or made money, his cheery temper always remained unruffled and unclouded. His popularity was great; and all his earlier ventures and activity were simply an apprenticeship for really large doings a little later.

I cannot say positively whether the embryo idea of a Jubilee emanated from him, or whether it took form from the chance suggestion of some one else; but I believe it to have been a Gilmore idea because of the peculiar make-up of the man. He was an earnest, loyal American. All the Southern States had come back into the fold, and we were once more a glorious Union. Peace and plenty reigned. Gilmore was just the sort of man into whose head would come buzzing the idea that the nation should have a big, rollicking family jubilee to celebrate the happy state of the country. Boston was the place above all places in which to hold it. It should be a musical and social reunion,—a magnificent *jubilate*. Such it was in reality.

Mr. Gilmore had the ability to inspire a very large number of people with a belief in him and his idea, who were willing to become financial guarantors. Accordingly a wooden building of good acoustic properties was promptly erected on the Back Bay lands, near or on the site of the present Art Museum,—a building capable of holding fifty thousand persons, including a big chorus of ten thousand and a great orchestra of one thousand. The audience was to be seated in chairs on a level, oblong floor and in the deep balcony which ran round the sides and the end facing the stage. A great organ was built for the occasion; also a bass drum, the head of which might have been ten or twenty feet in diameter. This drum was a special point of attraction; it seemed as big as a Fourth of July balloon.

The musical part of the Jubilee—all things considered,—was noble and dignified. The great chorus, the great orchestra, the great organ, the great drum, and the great singer, Parepa-Rosa, with her wonderful, never-to-be-forgotten rendering of the *Inflammatus*, may seem, at this distance of time and development of musical taste, as something only "great" to laugh at. Yet, when a whole serious-minded community like that of Boston "took stock" in it, and the spirit of the idea was carried out happily, is it not perhaps rash to mock at it? Have not the results been far-reaching, doing their work in this world of evolution just as the chromo prepares the way for high art? Who can say that a large share of Boston's musical reputation was not earned by the Jubilees?

Returning to details, it will surprise many to know that the orchestra numbered quite a thousand—with the patriotic Ole Bull at the head of the violins, and Carl Rosa playing at the same desk. Gilmore had engaged all the principal sopranos of Boston, constituting a "bouquet of artistic singers." These were placed on a special raised balcony between the orchestra and the chorus, and they sang in unison the *obligato* parts as they occurred in the choral pieces.

Great care had been exercised all through the preceding winter in preparing the choristers, who were scattered all over New England,—every village and town contributing a quota. They were supplied with the Jubilee music, and the leaders and directors of all these people had the *tempi* (Italian plural for "time") given them. During many months it was a busy time for Carl Zerrahn, as general music director, and his aids. They had to travel from town to town to drill the choristers,

PAREPA-ROSA. *Page* 191

or to see that the preparations were going on auspiciously.

When all the singers finally came together the result was pretty good. But a chorus of ten thousand persons would naturally occupy a wide space, and they would inevitably drag the *tempo*. Mr. Zerrahn often had to show good generalship by rushing up the aisle which separated the two divisions of the big choral army in order to get near enough to beat the laggards into time.

Mr. Gilmore was a modest and a wise man, and conducted but little of the music himself; but that little was great,—for did he not direct the "Anvil Chorus"? Will Boston, or at least its Jubilee participators, ever forget the sensation it had when the one hundred firemen—each in his belt, helmet, and red flannel shirt, carrying a long-handled blacksmith's hammer at "right shoulder shift" like a musket—marched into the hall and on to the stage in two files of fifty, and then separated far enough to form a red frame for two sides of the orchestra, which meanwhile was playing the introduction to the "Anvil Chorus"? Reaching their special, *real* anvils, the firemen faced the audience, lifted their hammers to the proper position, and at the right musical moment of time began to pound the anvils,—right, left, right, left,—while the great orchestra and chorus played and sang the melody.

If ever "the welkin rang" it did then!

In addition to the sounds from a hundred anvils there was the great organ, military band, drum corps, all the bells in the city achime, and a cannon accompaniment. This last came from two batteries of well served guns stationed at a short distance from the building, and a gun was fired off by electricity on the first beat of each measure. A small table was placed on the stage, close to the director, with a set of electric buttons, each having a wire leading to a gun. Mr. John Mullaly was the artist who pressed the button; the gun did the rest. These guns were similarly used for all national airs.

At the termination of the "Anvil Chorus" there was enormous applause. The whole mass of people rose to their feet, jumped up and down, and nearly dislocated their arms by waving handkerchiefs, fans, hats, parasols, even babies. I am sure that I was never in any great assembly where such wild, almost frantic cheering and applause was heard. Fifty thousand people in a wooden building can make some noise.

The dear, wonderful old *maestro*, Verdi, did certainly furnish a great opportunity for P. S. Gilmore. It is equally certain that Verdi never dreamed of the possibilities contained in the "slam-bang" popular melody. When the piece was ended, the gentlemen firemen would march out; and, the applause continuing, they would march back again and go through the whole exciting performance once more.

During the festival, some of the composers like J. K. Paine and Dudley Buck directed their own compositions. Mr. Eben Tourjée directed *Nearer, my God, to Thee*, and other hymn tunes.

This first festival was held in June, 1869, and lasted a week. Performances were given afternoons only,—nothing in the evenings, except a large, very successful ball given on Friday evening. People poured in from all parts of the country; distance was no hindrance,—they came from the far West and even from California.

On June 17th, the President of the United States, General Ulysses S. Grant, with Admiral Farragut, Admiral Thatcher, Commodore Winslow, a numerous staff, and the Governor of the State, all in full uniform, were present at the performance.

The financial part of the Jubilee was satisfactory. There was a very large income, $290,000, and a correspondingly large outlay, $283,000. All professional people, except the few who declined to receive pay, were paid. The care of the finance had been taken off Mr. Gilmore's shoulders. After every bill was paid, a respectable balance remained. This balance, together with the proceeds of a benefit concert, $32,000, making together $39,000, was, very properly and very handsomely, handed to Mr. Gilmore.

For musical completeness I give the programme of the first concert, June 15, 1869, which will serve as a type of all.

1. GRAND CHORAL, "A Strong Castle is our Lord,"
   Luther.
2. TANNHAUSER OVERTURE, Select Orchestra of 600,
   Wagner.
   Directed by Mr. JULIUS EICHBERG.
3. GLORIA from the Twelfth Mass, . . *Mozart.*
4. AVE MARIA, ... *Bach-Gounod.*
   Sung by Madame PAREPA-ROSA.
   The violin obligato played by two hundred violinists.
5. NATIONAL AIR, " The Star Spangled Banner," *Key.*
   Sung and played by the entire force with
   Bells and Cannon.

Intermission fifteen minutes.

6. AMERICAN HYMN, ... *Keller.*
7. OVERTURE, "William Tell." . . . *Rossini.*
8. INFLAMMATUS from the "Stabat Mater," *Rossini.* Madame PAREPA-ROSA.
9. CORONATION MARCH, from "Le Prophete," 1000 performers, ... *Meyerbeer.*
10. ANVIL CHORUS, from "Il Trovatore," . *Verdi.*
All the forces; 100 anvils, performed on by 100 members of the Boston Fire Department; Bells and Cannons.
11. MY COUNTRY, 'T IS OF THEE, words by REV. S. F. SMITH, D.D. All the forces; the audience requested to join in singing the last stanza.

CHAPTER XXIII

THE second Jubilee was held in 1872, and, like all repetitions of a similar nature, it was found to be impossible to get up a popular excitement equal to that which attended the first one. It was therefore not a financial success. The new building designed for it, and everything else, was on a larger scale, and not so easily handled. There were some notably fine features, but the whole was less of a strictly home affair.

Gilmore's plans again showed his genius. They were bold, well conceived, but very costly. He went to Europe, and "talked the crowned heads" (that was the popular phrase) "into letting their crack" military bands come over to play in the Jubilee. He obtained the band of the Grenadier Guards from London, about forty-five strong, under Dan Godfrey; a German infantry band, about thirty-five men, under Saro; and that of the Garde Républicaine, from Paris, of about fifty-five men. It was said that this latter was reinforced by fine artists from the opera, and was not therefore a fair sample of French bands. There was also a little insignificant band, the Royal Constabulary, from Ireland.

These bands had an English day and German, French, and Irish days. The English band was good, the German, too brassy, the French, magnificent. The latter opened with Meyerbeer's "Torch-Light Dance" (*Fackeltänze*) and won instant success. They had a double quartette of saxophones, four fagotti, a double fagott, and some very large tubas: and the total result was so round, full, and soft, that all musicians were captivated with the deep diapason volume of sound. Their performance of the *William Tell* overture was superb.

It is to be remembered that, in 1872, the political antagonism between the French and Germans was great. The Franco-Prussian War had left rankling hatred between the two peoples. The sight of a German to a Frenchman was like shaking a red rag in the face of a bull; consequently, on the day the French band of La Garde Républicaine marched down the broad aisle in full uniform, surrounded (in their imagination) by their enemies, the German musicians, it was certainly an anxious moment for the Frenchmen. It seemed to me—perhaps it was the effect of the sympathetic current created by the situation—that they were pale with anxiety. It was to be their battle-field; they were to be judged by prejudiced listeners, and they were on their mettle.

The performance of the band was musically so perfect that all prejudice was annihilated. Metaphorically the Germans embraced the Frenchmen; we were all of one brotherhood —politics and race differences had vanished— the music had disarmed all evil spirits. We were simply musicians, ready to award praise to merit. When the band ended the overture, the players all about them were as wild in their applause as the general public. And I am sure I saw some of the Frenchmen wipe away tears of joy at their well-won victory.

Mr. Gilmore had captured several rare lions and lionesses for his musical menagerie, chief among whom was the royal lion, Johann Strauss,—the famous waltz-composer from Vienna,—and Madame Peschka-Leutner, a colorature singer of extraordinary ability. This lady captivated her audiences with her clear, telling, high, and powerful soprano voice, her almost matchless execution, style, and other rare vocal gifts. She was a genuine success.

Then there was Madame Rudersdorf, a

JOHANN STRAUSS. *Page* 201

splendid singer, of broad, classic, oratorio style. She was of great value to the city of Boston, for she settled there and became a teacher of teachers.

Strauss, violin in hand, conducted the orchestra daily, in one of his most popular waltzes, and also in some little knick-knacks, such as the *Pizzicato Polka*, which became at once a great favorite. His manner of conducting was very animating. He led off with the violin bow to give the *tempo*, but when the right swing was obtained and the melody was singing out from the orchestra, he joined in with his fiddle as if he *must* take part in the intoxication of the waltz. While playing or conducting he commonly kept his body in motion, rising and falling on his toes in a really graceful manner.

It was natural that Strauss, the composer of the *Blue Danube*, should be an object of great interest to a large part of mankind and womankind. The man who had furnished the human family so many blissful moments, was bound to be an idol; and he had worship enough during the limited time allotted him to face his new-made Boston admirers. We must not forget that on all public parades he had his valet with him,—in gorgeous livery, a cockade on his hat, a brown and golden belt round his waist, a heavy cloth coat on, and over his arm (with the mercury at 90) a heavy cloak to place round his master, the king of waltz-makers, in case of need. This warmly dressed, though picturesque valet, always stood just at the front edge of the stage with his eyes fastened on his master. Some cynic has said, " No man is a hero to his valet." I take no more stock in that saying, for I think Strauss was a hero to his. We must judge somewhat by appearances in this world, as they often furnish our only ground for judgment.

This second Jubilee had a "coda," or tail, in the shape of a financial deficit, but the noble army of martyr guarantors "faced the music" like men.

Mr. Gilmore reached the apogee of his greatness at the period of these festivals. To conceive and carry out such plans showed much forethought and executive ability. First, to get those large military bands over from Europe—foreseeing that it would set the European world to talking of Gilmore and his band—was a pretty big thing; and then to follow it up (after he moved to New York City) by actually taking his New York band over to Great Britain, France, Germany, and

(I think) Italy, was certainly not only bearding the lion in his den, or carrying coals to Newcastle, but it was undertaking a financial venture of the most uncertain kind—and yet Mr. Gilmore, with clear vision of success in his eyes, boldly carried out the project, and returned from Europe with all his colors flying.

I think it can be seen that the brave, loyal bandmaster, Patrick Sarsfield Gilmore, filled a good page in the musical and social history of our country. We hopefully believe he now rests in peace.

CHAPTER XXIV

RUBINSTEIN and Wieniawski were, in my humble opinion, the two greatest artists who have up to date visited the United States. They came together, under some forgotten manager, and travelled a part of two seasons in 1873-74. Before and since the coming of Wieniawski we have had many fine violinists, beginning with Sivori, and followed by Ole Bull, Miska Hauser, Vieuxtemps, Sauret, Madame Camille Urso, Dangremont, Paul Jullien, — then Wieniawski, Wilhelmj, and quite recently Sarasate. Speaking from an entirely unbiassed standpoint, I say that Wieniawski overtopped them all. I think there was not one in the above list who could do certain things he did. In his *Carnaval de Venise*, he exhibited a mastery over every form of violin technics which quite reached the marvellous. His chromatic scale, played *staccato* from the lowest to the highest note, and down again to the lowest, in one bow,— either an up or down bow,— was a feat, a *tour*

HENRI WIENIAWSKI.

de force, shown us by no other virtuoso. His double trills and double harmonics were perfect. Nor was it in mere technical playing that he was great, for he played with much sentiment and feeling, and in quartette playing he showed his best quality. He was the master-player and king of all I have heard; Joachim alone excepted when playing Beethoven or Bach.

I have reserved my little talk about Rubinstein, not because he was the lesser of the two remarkable men,—for we all know he was the greater,—but Rubinstein, the pianist and composer, is not a subject to be disposed of in a few qualifying remarks. Doubtless there are partisans of various pianists, prepared to dispute my estimate of him and give battle at once. But let us not forget that a large proportion of persons is always satisfied that the latest good thing is the best in history. Also, it is fair to say there is quite as large a proportion, perhaps a larger one, which says that the old way or person is the best.

Luckily for the pianistic and musical world in general, the fact of Rubinstein's great playing is still attested by large numbers, and, we may add, by exclusively musical people. A considerable share of the partisanship of the present day is recruited from the ranks of society people, who take up people and *fads* and carry them till the next new, good thing comes; but the whole critical musical world has sung the praises of Rubinstein, from his advent as a player till the day of his death, with scarcely a dissenting voice. It is therefore fair to believe that it was not without reason that Europe had weighed him in the pianistic scales and agreed that he was the great master.

Let us add to that fact that he can be numbered among the creator-gods of music. Do not such beings possess an insight into the spirit and wishes even of other composers, not shared by those who have not the special gift of composition? Are not men like Rubinstein made to glow with a composer's rapture? We all remember how he used to thunder on the piano at times, and hit many wrong notes, and we knew the cause. His passion was roused —the brain working— the heart throbbing—his mental vision following the guiding spirit and the soul of the music. He was being carried on its wings into ethereal regions. At such moments, when cool mastery of technics was absent, his fingers would play him tricks. Even then it was a delight to be a listener, a joy to be a musician and be brought under the spell of his magic power.

ANTON RUBINSTEIN.

On one memorable occasion Rubinstein and Wieniawski did me the honor to spend an evening at my house in Boston. A right royal musical evening it was, shared by about fifty artist and amateur guests. We made much music,—beginning with Rubinstein's String Quintette in F, *op*. 57. Then we had the Rasoumoffski Quartette in F, *op*. 57, by Beethoven, with Wieniawski playing first violin. Then the Schumann Piano Quintette, with Rubinstein at the piano. Oh, it was a joy to take part with such a man and in such a work! and how Rubinstein did spur us on by his passionate way of playing some of the great parts! his power was fierce and tremendous. I think we all revelled in the sea of sound we made about us.

After the Quintette, Rubinstein played a lot of choice solo pieces, ending the evening with the Chopin Polonaise in A flat, *op*. 53, in which comes the wonderful passage for the left hand in octaves. He began the phrase very soft, then the "little-by-little *crescendo*" was most admirably done, finally reaching a *fortissimo* power which was quite colossal. It stirred us all up, and set even the chandelier to jingling in sympathy, and possibly in admiration.

It may not be amiss to give a little incident showing Rubinstein's frank, lovable personality. On the evening of the above *musicale*, we had planned to make an intermission after the second composition, to rest the artists and allow an opportunity for people to meet Rubinstein. No sooner had we ended the Quartette than Rubinstein came to me and asked if he could not go down-stairs and smoke a cigarette. I said, "Yes, certainly"; and we went down to the dining-room, where we discovered that the table was spread for the supper. Rubinstein at once said, "I must not smoke here; can't we go into the kitchen?" "Of course," said I; so we plunged into the kitchen. This important part of the premises we found in possession of three colored men of the well-known J. B. Smith, caterer, and the atmosphere was frightfully hot. The next question from Rubinstein was, couldn't he take off his coat, it was so warm? Off came the coat, followed by the remark that it was just delightful to enjoy the freedom of a home, and how often had he gone into his own kitchen to have a smoke! While he was in the midst of the sacred indulgence, Mrs. Ryan came to the door searching for Rubinstein, in order to introduce him to some of the friends. The instant she appeared he got into his coat with the celerity of a theatrical expert, took one more puff at the cigarette, and was ready for duty.

I often recall the trifling episode,—Rubinstein and I seated near the door farthest from the cooking-range, he in shirt-sleeves with his coat spread on his knees, and the three colored men busy at the range but often turning round to stare at the stranger with his odd ways, language, and gestures.

Rubinstein's character was simple and unaffected, interesting and individual, throughout.

CHAPTER XXV

FROM the time of closing up the National College of Music in 1873, the Mendelssohn Quintette Club travelled season after season, giving concerts in all parts of the country.

When we began going West in 1862 or 1863, towns like Indianapolis, St. Paul, Grand Rapids, and Cleveland, were small; and we have seen them grow into large, populous cities, and noticed the changes in the manners and customs of the people. There is very little difference now in the people of any section; they are so homogeneous that we cannot tell whether we are playing in Bangor or Omaha or on the Pacific Coast. We have frequently visited Canada, from Newfoundland to British Columbia.

In the early spring of 1881, we made our first visit to California, and how new and romantic it did seem! We were not so *blasé* as we became afterwards.

I knew that in San Francisco I was to meet many old friends, and I realized most of my pleasant anticipations. We left Omaha behind us in snowdrifts, just as we had left all nature in the Eastern and Middle States in the desolation of winter storms. These same storms followed us till we reached Reno, in Nevada. Waking up the next morning in Sacramento, California—what a change! The jump from winter to summer had been made in one day-and-night's journey. All nature had put on the lovely dress of June. The odor of flowers, the distinctive feature of California, was in the atmosphere we breathed, and the delight from it was throbbing within us, when, as if to emphasize our joy, one of the expected friends came to the train to meet myself and my family, bringing a great mass of roses freshly gathered from his garden. How wonderful and delightful it did seem!

We all get accustomed to this kind of thing in time, and it no longer stirs our enthusiasm. But the first experience stays by one as a charming souvenir.

Our concert experience in California was pleasant and profitable. We visited nearly every place up and down the coast, including Oregon and Washington Territory. In San Francisco we gave an extended set of concerts, and when leaving for Australia we had a farewell which made us all happy. The Quintette Club at that time was composed of the following artists: First violin, Isidor Schnitzler; second violin, August Thiele; flute and viola, William Schade; clarinet and viola, Thomas Ryan; violoncello, Fritz Giese; Miss Miller, soprano.

While we were in "Frisco," we had been advised that a concert trip to Australia would be a profitable one, and we determined to undertake it. It was a bold venture. The cost of fares one way for agent and company was fourteen hundred dollars. There was a chance that we might have to "come home on our trunks" (in theatrical parlance); yet we were quite sure we could not "foot it." It is a pity that slang alone can paint the possible situation.

Steamers for Australia sailed only once a month. Our agent went a month in advance of us, taking a good stock of printed matter to prepare the way. The voyage from "Frisco" to Sydney takes twenty-eight days. We were advertised to start on a Saturday, and our Club was to give a concert in Honolulu the following Saturday; but the English mails were late in reaching "Frisco," and we could not sail till Sunday. That fact unfortu-

THE MENDELSSOHN QUINTETTE CLUB THAT WENT TO AUSTRALIA, 1881.

nately prevented our reaching Honolulu till the Sunday following, and we gave no concert till we made the return trip, ten months later.

We had a pleasant and uneventful voyage on the steamer *Zelandia*. It is just one week's sail to Honolulu. The ship requires about ten hours to unload and load. The next port made is Auckland, in New Zealand, fourteen days' sail, where a stop of from six to eight hours is made. The next port is Sydney, in New South Wales, seven days' sail, and the end of the trip.

After a few days' rest and a chance to get our fingers into working order, we gave a *soirée*, by invitation, in Pahling's piano warerooms, to newspaper and music people. The papers declared that nothing so thoroughly artistic as our Club had hitherto visited their colony. It was a good send-off.

Throughout the colonies our system of giving concerts was very different from that in vogue in the United States. We generally hired a hall or opera house for two weeks, and played nightly, giving more classic music than we would then have dared to play at home. Generally there were four different prices for admission, ranging from one to four or five shillings. Very many people bought their tickets at the doors with bank checks. I have often had as many as fifty of these little checks on different banks, the amounts ranging from two shillings to a pound. It was a nice little job each morning to get them cashed.

About four days before we sailed from San Francisco, the shooting of President Garfield had occurred. At Honolulu we could hear no report of the good man's condition. Fourteen days later, on arriving at Auckland, the American consul came to the ship to give us the joyful news that Garfield was out of danger, and would probably "pull through." That was a cheering send-off for the next trip of seven days. But alas! on the morning following our arrival at Sydney came the very sad news of his death. Genuine sorrow was felt by the citizens of Sydney; the stores were closed, all business was stopped, and a public meeting was called in the City Hall. All Americans were present and many speeches of condolence were made by sympathizers. We were made to realize that in the branches of the English-speaking race a strong relationship exists; hit one member of the family hard, and you hit all.

When I sailed away from America's shores my good wife insisted that I should contribute a letter once a month for the Boston *Transcript*. I wrote five such letters, from which I quote freely in the following account of our Australian experiences.

After our arrival in Sydney and the *soirée* by invitation, we gave concerts in the City Hall for two weeks. We also made a trip into Queensland, stopping first at Brisbane, the capital of the colony, five hundred miles north of Sydney, on the coast. Most of our travelling was by water, as we only visited the cities, and they lay on the fringe of the continent. We became pretty good sailors, and thought no more of a voyage of from two to seven days than we would of a trip from Boston to Springfield or Portland by rail. On the voyage to Brisbane we sailed most of the time within a few miles of the shore, and could see that the country was almost a wilderness, covered with eucalyptus trees, of the prevailing olive-green color. Two days' sail brought us to Brisbane, a city with a population of thirty thousand. We underwent the doctor's inspection, and then put up at a comfortable hotel. We gave about seven concerts, then took steamer for Maryborough, twenty-four hours distant.

Early on the morning of the next day some aborigines came on board from an island ; real natives,—six men and three women—a mean lot. The women were in full, extra gala travelling costume (and I was given to understand were in deep mourning). Their heads were decorated with a mass of small copper-colored feathers, gummed to their hair, over which was a rag of a handkerchief which, keeping all in place, was tied under the chin. One young woman was extra gay. Her dress consisted of an old Balmoral skirt, held with a string going up over the left shoulder, crossing the back, and meeting the skirt again under the right arm. This picturesque arrangement left both arms, and, in fact, the whole body, quite unfettered. I was told (it may have been a libel, though) that on their reservations, mainly islands, their costume consists of the feathers only. The other two women were dressed a little more in the fashion of the day. They had cotton gowns on, docked rather short it is true, and ragged and torn, but that simply took away a certain otherwise inevitable stiffness. The gowns were fresh from the ash-pit, that was certain; no poor laundress had to suffer from their exacting ideas of nicety. They all wore the hosiery Nature gave them, their shoes were untanned except by the sun, and—oh, poor creatures!—such thin shanks!

Bread and meat were given them. Charming was it to see their mutual friendliness. A large bone, with plenty of meat, was in the hands of one of the party; he or she would take a good generous mouthful from the bone, then pass it to the next, and so on. When they had polished the bones and were satisfied, they squatted on the poop-deck and began playing cards, each chipping in a penny for the pool. They grew very excited over the loss of a trick, and it was a severe struggle every time, both with cards and tongue, to get the pool.

The gentlemen of this party had to work their passage, cleaning brasses, unloading cargo, etc. They were all of a dark negro color, with a very mean, despicable look, such as you see sometimes in a cur dog; they drink to excess. Up-country here, they always have dogs with them. Men and women, always in Indian file, follow each other,—never two together,—always scolding and quarrelling. The women often carry a scanty little wardrobe, blanket, etc., on a clothesline which, put round the neck, hangs down their backs—baby thrown in. They are all beggars in towns, and are not allowed to sleep within the precincts; they stretch out anywhere, the climate being merciful. Speaking of climate in Queensland, it may be summed up as fine. We are now only two hundred miles from the Tropic of Capricorn. The sun shines hot, but the atmosphere is never debilitating. Miasma and malaria are totally unknown.

In Maryborough we gave four concerts, doing a fair business. By rail we went sixty miles in the interior to Gympie, a mining-town on the hills. As they never have frost, the bulk of miners live in little huts of bark, or tents, and can sleep out of doors the year round. Indeed, beds for extra guests in hotels are made up on verandas and piazzas.

Our concert room here is the Variety Theatre, a fair-sized barn, with doors on hinges up near the roof, opening for light and air. The sides are of weather-boards only, the roof shingled withth in hardwood, no lining; stars shine through; and as people commonly carry umbrellas, they are prepared to use them in case of a sudden shower. The night of the first concert, we had in the shilling part—rear end of the barn—about two hundred people, mostly miners. These gentlemen were prepared to enjoy the concert in their own way, nearly every one having a good honest clay pipe. The little wax matches which light with a snapping noise were going all the time,— you could plainly see the spark on the background of good thick smoke. As we had a large front part of house at four and three shillings, I made up my mind to try the effect of a coaxing appeal to the gentlemen in the rear to abstain from smoking. I spoke of the heat, close air, the general enjoyment which all would realize if they would abstain from smoking while the performances went on. It had the desired effect: they put up their pipes, were very quiet, attentive, and enthusiastic; but when approaching the end of part first, we could hear the little explosive matches on all sides going like fireworks, and at the last note up rose nearly every man, with a good head of pipe on, and marched out the side door, to take the air, and "see a friend."

We usually allow nearly fifteen minutes between parts; our agent rings a bell out-of-doors like the schoolmarm, and in they troop.

CHAPTER XXVI

AFTER our venture in Queensland we returned to Sydney and prepared for our trip to Tasmania, formerly named Van Diemen's Land,—an island about two hundred miles long and shaped like a crusader's shield. It was three days' sail from New South Wales. We reached Hobart, the capital of the colony, situated at its southern extremity, on December 24th. Steaming into the bay on a lovely early summer morning, the view was enchanting. On the left of the bay, rising from a beautiful sandy beach, stands Mount Nelson, twelve hundred feet high, with a very picturesque flag station on the summit. At the right of the bay, at the base of a hill, is Battery Point, a rounded eminence of greensward. Between these two points lies snugly ensconced the town, which spreads up and over the slopes of numerous small hills having for background a high hill, densely wooded, then a deep valley, and then, to crown the picture, directly in the centre, Mount Wellington, 4166 feet high. The

HOBART, TASMANIA.

whole make-up of bay, shipping, handsome buildings, and embowered dwellings, with an old-fashioned red brick windmill on a hill, its skeleton arms, now unused, stretching out, made a picture more attractive than any my eyes ever rested on—and further acquaintance with the town but increased its charm for me.

There are the usual recreation-grounds for the people, a beautiful demesne on the edge of the bay; a good-sized historical museum, containing valuable coins, birds, beasts, fishes, and geological specimens found in the colonies; a large public library, and handsome town hall, where we played,—which, by the way, has three glass chandeliers worthy to be placed in a Parisian opera house. In the centre of a pretty garden square stands a handsome bronze statue of Sir John Franklin, who was one of the former governors. There is also a fine botanic garden of rare trees, fruits, and flowers.

The day following our arrival being Christmas Day, we duly celebrated it by making up a party of four Americans, including Professor Denton of Boston (the lecturer on geology, who had just concluded a series of lectures), to "do" Mount Wellington. It proved to be a very fatiguing tramp of twenty-one miles there and back, but richly were we rewarded.

Part of the way up a very steep trail, when nearing the summit, we had about a quarter of a mile of the roughest kind of climbing, over what is called the "ploughed fields," made up of huge, basaltic, columnar rocks, which formerly were the face of the mountain, and in falling were shattered, crushed, wedged in, and then rounded in time by the elements. This struggle over, we were fairly on the table-land.

Another one and a half miles brought us to the looking-off place, the view from which was certainly grand beyond description. The day was warm and perfect, the atmosphere clear. We could see about ninety miles distant, over nearly three fourths of the horizon. It was a beautiful intermingling of land and sea,—innumerable bays making in from the ocean, some with bluffy margins, others with lovely sweeps of half-moon beaches; all wonderfully fascinating, the sea being of a very light blue and the breakers on the bright sand beaches making a uniform fringe of pure white, marrying exquisitely with the background of thickly wooded shores. These beautiful effects of color and shape made us fairly wild with delight. Then there were various narrow arms of the sea making into the land, which, sloping off gently on both sides to the water, gave promise of opportunity in the coming years for homes fit for a race of artist-kings. Indeed, we all agreed that if Tasmania were part of Northeastern America, it would speedily become one of the greatest watering-places, in the finest sense, in the world. From our objective point we could look down on the streets of Hobart, the harbor, and about twenty miles up the Derwent River.

We gave ten concerts in Hobart (population about twenty thousand), all well attended, with one great crowd on the night of a concert given under the patronage of the new governor. All the fashion, of necessity, were out. Leaving this cozy city, we took train for Launceston, the only other city in the colony, stopping to give one concert each at Oatlands and Campbelltown. This latter place is the town to which the American government sent a body of astronomers to observe the transit of Venus a few years since. These two little places, each of about one thousand population, gave us crowds. They came in from long distances.

Launceston, with a population of about twelve thousand, has not the natural beauties of Hobart, but is nevertheless a handsome town, built upon the sides of a hill, and is the centre of a fine farming country—farms resembling those seen in Vermont—with plenty of fat cattle and thousands of sheep. Two rivers, the North and South Esk, here join and form the Tamar, —a pretty harbor for shipping. The South Esk is for many miles a swift cataract, running through a gorge in the mountains filled with wild, picturesque beauty. Where it debouches into the Tamar, it is spanned from hill to hill by a light iron bridge two hundred feet long and of a single arch, forming a very graceful object in the landscape.

In Launceston we gave five evening concerts of mixed music and one matinée of classic, to large and enthusiastic audiences. In both cities they have musical associations which give oratorios; though I noticed that in one of the cities there is a professor who advertises to "teach singing and music." One delightful souvenir of Launceston I shall not soon forget,—the charming hospitality of a most remarkable woman, between sixty and seventy years of age, authoress, poetess, and accomplished artist, married early in life in England, her husband high in government life. She has written a series of works describing Tasmania, illustrated by her pencil in quite a wonderful way; and her abundant means enabled her to have them printed in London for private distribution. While still a girl, living in Birmingham, England, in 1833 Paganini, the great, visited that city. A few verses of poetic rapture on hearing him play brought him to her feet. He expressed his homage by presenting her a silhouette picture, with a suitable dedication in his own handwriting, on a page in an album, on the opposite page of which the great man wrote the first eight measures of the *Campanella Rondo* for violin. My delight and surprise at seeing such a souvenir in so remote a quarter of the globe may be easily imagined by musicians.

The history of Tasmania is full of interest, made so chiefly by the fact that all the deported criminals formerly in Botany Bay were carried to that island. That act, joined to the "wiping out" (so to characterize it) of the native population, has created a page of history as savage as it is romantic. I can add to that history a few facts quite in keeping with the general trend of Tasmania's records.

When I was a boy of perhaps six years of age, my father's regiment was stationed in Plymouth, England. An order came from the government that two soldiers from each infantry regiment could volunteer to go to

Tasmania. They must however be married men and each have at least two children. On arriving at the colony, they would receive their free discharge, a tract of land, and some money to help them to start in the new life. The government's plan was to have in that colony a force of men suitable to do police duty. I remembered that two men volunteered from our regiment.

On my arrival in Hobart, the capital of the colony, I sought information about these old volunteers; I had remembered the name of one of them, and that was a help in getting on to their traces. I quickly ascertained that one of them was dead, and the other was a poor imbecile in a distant asylum. Their families had quite disappeared from the island.

CHAPTER XXVII

ON January 19, 1882, we returned to Sydney and made a short tour in the interior of the colony. While on this trip I was fated to have a personal experience as strange as anything to be found in a novel.

Just before I was married in 1854, a brother of my future wife was induced by some young men of his own age to try his fortunes in Australia. The reports of the gold "finds" in that country were more attractive even than those coming from California.

The party sailed from New York in one of the American clipper ships for the city of Melbourne, and presumably arrived in safety; but, though my wife wrote many letters to her brother, in the care of the American consul, no replies ever reached us. Year after year rolled by, with its growing uneasiness concerning the fate of the gold-seeker, till, finally, in the twenty-eighth year of his absence an intimate friend going to Australia promised faithfully to aid us, and did ascertain that the brother had been dead for several years, leaving a widow and one child, and that he had been reputed to be a wealthy man. We wrote to the widow, but no reply came; Australia, like the United States, is a big country. Part of my object in visiting those distant colonies was to find that widow, but up to the time of our arrival in New South Wales, I had made no movement in that direction, for I was awaiting our visit to the colony of Victoria, when I meant to visit the Ballarat region.

On this trip we arrived towards evening in a small town where we were to give a concert. I was met by our agent at the railroad station, who told me that the proprietress of the hotel was a relative of mine, and was very anxious to meet me. Approaching the house, I saw a lady waiting on the piazza. The agent introduced me by name. She was strangely agitated, and asked me if I did not once have a brother-in-law in the colony. I replied, " No; I did have one in Victoria, but he is no longer alive, and I intend to search out his widow when I visit Victoria." The lady said, " I knew the husband intimately and also the widow." I asked, " What kind of woman is the widow, and can you tell me where I can find her?" She replied, " She is not far to seek and is a good woman." Instantly I exclaimed, "Then you are the widow?" "Yes," was the reply, in broken tones.

A young lady, under twenty years of age, then came forward, and was introduced as her daughter, who had recently been married. Both mother and daughter were greatly affected. After a while I was able to learn their histories.

The dead husband was a thorough American; he had worked in the mines, carried on a sizable hotel, and had made a good deal of money. Meantime his health failed; in short, he was consumptive. The wife urged him to make a trip to the United States, to see his relations once more, and then return. Deciding to carry out this plan, he had a special carriage made for his comfort by which to go to Melbourne, about two hundred miles distant. An American was selected to travel with him, and a large sum of money in cash and drafts, sufficient for the entire trip, was drawn from the bank.

The sick man started on his long journey, in very dejected spirits. On the second day a telegram reached the wife to the effect that she must hasten to a town *en route* if she wanted to see her husband alive. She started at once, but he had passed away from this life before she could reach him. Very little of the money he had taken was found on his person; the people round him declared it must have been stolen while he lay asleep the first night.

The usual troubles followed,—the return *cortège* to the desolate home, the law settlements, etc. After all expenses and debts were paid, not much ready money was left, and of real estate only the hotel. The lady remained a widow for several years; then she realized that a husband would be a great help, and was married to a good man.

A few years were passed in comfort—then dire misery again supervened. The hotel, which was a wooden-frame building, took fire and was destroyed. The wife saved some personal effects, — among them the former husband's old American trunk, which had always stood on the piazza outside their door. When trying to save things from the flames, she happened to notice it, gave it a shove, and it fell to the ground. It was saved to furnish a pathetic proof of the vicissitudes which can attend the life of a poor old American trunk. It had now one badly charred end, and the body of it barely held together.

Another thing saved was a lady's hat-box in which were letters written to the brother and his widow by my wife, also a few *carte-de-visite* pictures which we had sent them from time to time. It was a singular collection and illustrated the story told me by the wife and daughter.

The latter showed me with great pride another thing she had managed to save from the fire, her father's old American-made guitar. He was a good player and used to play accompaniments for the little daughter's singing; so her first instinct on the night of the fire was to save the old guitar. As she told me the story she took up the old instrument, put her arms round it, and embraced and kissed it as if in affectionate remembrance of her father.

This long story was told after our evening concert, and I wrote it down in black and white, not daring to trust it to memory, and mailed the record to my family.

To return to our travels, we gave a farewell concert at Sydney which was very gratifying. The music-lovers had decorated the stage with flowers and large English and American flags. Enthusiasm quite reached fever-heat when, at the right moment, a lady came on the stage and handed me, as conductor of the Club, two very beautiful flags, English and American, made of satin, and fully three feet long, with an inscription in silver letters wishing us all " good luck."

The next day we sailed for Melbourne, the Mecca of our pilgrimage, five hundred miles distant. We spent a month delightfully in that city, which we found to be a musical one, if several musical societies and many concerts are good proof of that statement.

We made our *début* in a concert given by the Apollo Club, a society built on the lines of that of Boston. It was for us a grand send-off. The conductor was Mr. Julius Herz, an enthusiastic and accomplished musician.

Another fine musician, conductor of the " Melbourne Club," was Mr. Julius Siede, with whom I was glad to meet and revive old memories. He had come to the United States with Gungl's Orchestra, and was a brilliant flautist. When that orchestra returned to Germany, Siede settled in New York, but afterward came to Boston. He then travelled to the antipodes with Madame Anna Bishop and Bochsa, the harpist. Siede finally made Melbourne his home. He was curious to know all about " the States," and we had many long talks before the time came for

FERN TREES, NEAR INVERCARGILL, NEW ZEALAND.

our club to leave the magnificent city of Melbourne.

We sailed to Adelaide, capital of South Australia, two days distant. It is a charming city with a population of fifty thousand. We gave about ten concerts, with fair success. We had there an experience of hot weather, never to be forgotten; for two days the mercury registered 120 degrees in the shade.

Returning to Melbourne, we had a splendid farewell concert in the grand City Hall. We were honored by the attendance of all the city dignitaries, in their regal robes. After the concert, the Club and the assisting artists were treated to a supper in the mayor's room. When parting-day came we bade good-bye with regret to the many Melbourne people who had become warm friends.

We were now to start on the home-stretch, —New Zealand being the point where we began to turn our faces toward America. We had a stormy sail of six days to reach Invercargill, the lowest point on the South Island.

I will give but a summary of our work in New Zealand: Three concerts in Invercargill, population 6000; ten in Dunedin, population 40,000; thirteen in Christchurch, population 28,000; six in Auckland, population 20,000.

In Dunedin (Scotch for Edinboro') we met with an old fellow-artist, Mr. Beno Schereck, who used to travel as pianist with Madame Camille Urso. In Christchurch (a city started by the Bishop of Canterbury) I had the pleasure of meeting Mr. Julius Haast, the curator of the great Museum. He had lived in the United States many years, and was famous for being the finder of the Moa bird.

On the trip to Auckland we stopped at Wellington, the capital of New Zealand. I had a note of introduction to Dr. Hector, the curator of the large Government Museum. He also had lived in the United States, and was a man of resolute character, happiest when he had some dangerous exploring trip on hand. I must repeat a story he told. He had been ordered by the government to visit the Maori country and examine a little lake singularly placed in the cup of what looked like an extinct crater, on quite a high mountain; the water of the lake having an issuance on the mountainside, far below its bottom, thence forming a river. The doctor's duty was to obtain from the Maoris permission to examine and measure it.

The mountain was in the heart of the Maori country, a sacred burial-place, and of course

STREET SCENE, DUNEDIN, NEW ZEALAND.

tabooed to all white people. After a long journey on horseback he reached the Pa (village) of the tribe, and requested its chiefs to permit him as government surveyor to make a drawing of the mountain lake. They told him they would consider the matter, call a meeting of the chiefs for the next evening, and then let him know their decision. The professor's time was valuable; he could n't wait for the Maori red tape to be measured, etc. Apparently acquiescing in the arrangements of the council, he spent the night quietly resting. Next morning he started out in an opposite direction to the mountain, went into the bush, found a secure hiding-place for his horse, tied him, made a détour on foot, climbed the sacred mountain, and made a satisfying drawing of the lake. It was a very risky thing to do. Returning to his horse and back to the village, he attended the meeting, and received permission, never before given to a white man, to visit the sacred spot; he then showed them his completed drawing. All they did was quietly to laugh over the affair.

I have seen goodly numbers of the Maoris on the coast steamers and in the streets of cities. Physically, they are a fine race,—tall and well formed. Only among the old men can one now see those whose faces are tattooed. Most of the women, young and old, are tattooed across the red of both lips, then incurved double lines toward the chin, meeting there, then a small device in the centre. The *ensemble* makes the impression of a faint goatee whisker, when seen from a little distance.

Four days' sail carried us to Auckland, where we gave six successful concerts. Then, on the 23d of May, we embarked on the noble steamship *City of New York*, flying the "Stars and Stripes," and commanded by the most fatherly of men, Captain Cobb; which in good time brought us to our homeland.*

En route, after a voyage of fourteen days, we stopped at Honolulu. It had been arranged for us to give a concert in that city if circumstances permitted. When our ship was approaching the shore, on June 5, 1882, but was still about two miles from the wharf, a fleet of small boats came out to meet friends, and from one of them came the questions, "Is the Quintette Club on board? Are they ready to give the concert?" To which we joyfully replied, "Yes." Thereupon, the boat signalled

---

* As before stated, these notes of travel in Australia, etc., are quoted from letters written at the time, and no attempt is made to bring them up to date.

the wharf, and the news was sent to the telephone office. Thence it was promptly speeded round the city, reserved seats were taken with a rush, and we had a fine audience. Nearly all the passengers on our ship, 250 in number, were present, as well as the best society in the place, including King Kalakaua and his court, crowding the boxes of the opera house. After the concert we were fêted by a German society at their club-rooms, where we "made a night of it," until it was time for the ship to sail, early next morning.

A voyage of seven days brought us to San Francisco. As we sailed through the Golden Gate, and I looked with mingled pride and pleasure on the familiar scenes, every object seemed to have a voice, and all sang to my ears, "Welcome home again," and I was glad.

When the Club made its first visit to California, our singer was Miss Marie Nellini, a brilliant singer, but a very poor sailor. When preparing for Australia, we were able to engage a good singer who was also a good sailor, Miss Cora Miller. On our return from Australia, I was introduced by Mrs. Rosewald, the well-known vocal teacher in San Francisco, to Marie Barnard. I discovered immediately that she was a genius in her line. She travelled with us for two seasons, and then went to Paris to prepare for the operatic stage. She has since developed into a good actress under the name of Marie Barna.

When leaving for Europe she promised to find a singer to replace her. In a very few weeks she cabled me, " Have found fine singer for you." In due season Miss Lila Juel arrived, young, tall, handsome, and a Swede. She sang with me for two years. It would be difficult to find a better concert singer or a more amiable person.

In 1862, Teresa Carreño, a remarkable child pianist, nine years of age, accompanied by her father and mother, came to the United States from Caracas, Venezuela.

The father of this "wonder child" was a man of distinguished political position in his country, and was also a devoted musical amateur. He was the child's only instructor up to her seventh year of age; then Julius Hoheni, a German professor, took charge of her. On the arrival of the family in New York, the distinguished pianist, Gottschalk, took the greatest interest in the little girl, gave her lessons, and taught her many of his brilliant pieces.

Teresa was gifted with a wonderful memory.

MISS LILA JUEL.

She could acquire the mastery of a lengthy, difficult *fantaisie* in two or three days. This gift is always the surest sign of a musical temperament that will bring distinction to its possessor.

Teresa made her first appearance in Boston, January 4, 1863. She remained here about one month, and was a great attraction at the grand orchestral concerts which were given at that period under the direction of Carl Zerrahn or P. S. Gilmore. She created a *furore* of enthusiasm every time she played. I doubt if any child pianist of the same age has ever exceeded her in ability. Imagine a child of nine years playing Thalberg's *Moses*, Gottschalk's *Jerusalem*, and similar pieces, full of technical difficulties.

Teresa was a lovable character, rather sedate and thoughtful, with very attractive features, beautiful, pleading eyes, and a strong and healthful physique. My family were greatly attracted to her. She and her mother, a large handsome woman, paid us several visits. Teresa never failed to bring her doll with her.

At the end of the Boston visit, Teresa gave what was termed a Juvenile Reception to at least three thousand school children in Music Hall. She wished distinctly to do this thing;

she said that being herself a child, she wanted the children of Boston to hear her. At this concert his Honor Mayor Cobb (I think it was) led Teresa on to the stage and made a little speech; then she played, to the children's great delight; after which came the reception, first in the anteroom, and then on the stage. It was with difficulty she could tear herself away from her young hearers.

Carreño's artistic life is well known in America, for though she paid many visits to her own country and Europe, a large part of her early life was spent among us. She can certainly be called American at least by adoption. As a pianist she has for years stood in the front rank of brilliant players. A few seasons ago she played the great No. 4 Concerto, by Rubinstein, in one of the Boston Symphony Concerts. I was one of the delighted listeners.

While she was thrilling me with her magnificent playing of the great composition, my mind was travelling back to her first appearance in that same Music Hall, when as a little child she had to climb upon the music stool to play her piece. After the concert I did myself the honor of visiting her. In conversation, we went over much that had happened in her art life. She, as a good American, wished to know all about the progress of music in the United States since she had made her home in Germany.

I regard her as a wonderful player in all respects. She is now in the prime of life, strong and vigorous, full of verve and intelligence, of fine mental grasp, and is as thoroughly devoted to her art as she was at twenty years of age. Her great popularity therefore is easily accounted for.

CHAPTER XXVIII

WHEN our club arrived in San Francisco from Australia in the summer of '82, we received a cable message from Mr. Henry E. Abbey, then in London, offering us an engagement to travel the coming season with Madame Christine Nilsson. It was joyfully accepted, and the season was one of the pleasantest we ever passed. We performed on the average three or four times each week, visiting only large cities East and West, and New Orleans and California. The company comprised: Madame Nilsson, soprano; Miss Hope Glen, alto (an American singer who has lived most of her time in London); Mr. Theodore Biorksten, tenor; Signor Del Puente, the well-known baritone; Mr. Charles Pratt, accompanist; and the Mendelssohn Quintette Club.

Madame Nilsson was in the prime of her vocal powers, and her renditions of the *Ah Perfido*, *Angels ever Bright and Fair*, and *Connais tu le pays*, were examples of great singing. Her *cheval de bataille*, however, was the "Jewel

CHRISTINE NILSSON.

Song" from *Faust*, by Gounod. She used to "go through all the motions," just the same as she would in opera. Her ballad singing was a revelation of the fine, tender heart she possessed. It was a rare occasion when she was not forced by popular desire to sing the *Suwanee River*. She doubtless will be remembered by the great mass of music-lovers as the lady who sang so touchingly about the "old folks at home."

Many people have an incorrect idea of Madame Nilsson's personality; it was popularly reported that she was cold, austere, distant, and unapproachable. As I had a rare opportunity to learn her true character, I can sum it up in a few words: in public and on the stage she was dignified and queen-like, but in private life she was full of geniality and amiability. As an example of her good-heartedness I will instance a pleasant evening she made for us on Christmas eve in Denver, Colorado.

During the day she sent for me and requested me to get the members of the company to meet together in her parlor at sharp nine in the evening, and confided to me her plans for their entertainment. Accordingly I saw them all and suggested that it would be a charming thing for us to surprise Nilsson with a Christmas-eve call; as fellow-artists she certainly would be delighted to see us. They thought it a good idea; and we called on her very near the appointed hour, each one entering singly, and expressing pleasure at meeting the others.

Nilsson carried out her part with the tact of a consummate actress, receiving each visitor with amiable and friendly greeting. Altogether there were eleven of us, besides the Danish minister and his wife. For a while we had a pleasant time chatting with our hostess and each other; then suddenly we heard three sharp knocks on the door,—bang–bang–bang,—and we all cried out, "Il Commendatore from Don Giovanni!"

"Mercy on us, what is that!" exclaimed Nilsson. Bang–bang–bang,—came three more knocks. "Won't some one go to the door?" she asked. "Such a knock as that on Christmas eve is rather terrifying."

I ran to the door, opened it cautiously, and then threw it wide open, disclosing to view two men with a great basket, big enough for the "buck-basket" in *Falstaff*. "Madame," I explained, "these men say they have been ordered to bring this basket to you, with Mr. Abbey's compliments."

The basket was set in the midst of the room; the lid was lifted; Nilsson went down beside it, and after removing a mass of paper and wrappings brought a lot of Christmas gifts to light,—one for each of the party, all duly marked in her own handwriting.

After these gifts had all been received, and inspected with much pleasure and merriment, Madame Nilsson said, " Mr. Ryan, please help me to put the basket outside the door"; and I ran to aid her. As we lifted it she said, "Why, I feel a great weight still; what can it be?" Dipping down deeper into the basket she brought up some very nice things to eat, and a goodly number of bottles of Golden-Seal champagne.

We drank to the health of everybody, our hearts grew light and merry, and the homesickness we felt at being away from home on Christmas eve was dispelled. It was in Nilsson's power, as the "star" of the company, to make us all happy, and most charmingly she did it. Her thoughtfulness on that occasion placed her very high in my estimation.

A few years later, we received another cable message from Mr. Henry E. Abbey, engaging our club to travel with the wonderful boy pianist, Otto Hegner. We opened the season with him in the Metropolitan Opera House in New York City. For that occasion, in addition to the Hegner company, a grand orchestra under Walter Damrosch was employed. The engagement lasted less than three months, for the "star boy-pianist," though acknowledged by the press to be a marvel for one so young, did not "take" well enough with the public to produce good financial results. It was therefore wise to end the tour as soon as the situation became evident.

In the previous year the little Josie Hoffmann, another boy pianist, had had an enormous success under Mr. Abbey's management, and a repetition of the same kind of performance is pretty sure to be a failure. The young Hegner was a perfect little darling, and yet a manly boy, of lovable disposition, entirely unaffected, unspoiled, tractable, and respectful to his father to a degree not generally found in such precocious folk. When he returned to Europe he was placed under competent masters for systematic study. The boy of yore has now grown to man's estate, and his genius is acknowledged, for he has played with success in the best concerts given in the capitals of Europe.

CHAPTER XXIX

A HISTORY of the incidents and happenings that our club met with while filling engagements would suffice to fill a book of respectable size. Some of them were exasperating, some were droll, and others were discouraging. But they were all "in the day's work," and helped to make up the life. I recall a few, which may serve as types of the numerous whole.

The first concert we ever gave in Topeka, Kansas, about thirty-five years ago, was signalized by a scene I shall not soon forget. We had a full house in the local concert hall. I noticed when we began to play that the front row of seats was empty, evidently reserved for some special people. Those "specials" came in while we played our first piece. They were Indians, about twelve in number, some being "blanket Indians"—which means that they wore their brilliant blue and yellow striped blankets shawl-wise, and their buckskin moccasins, and that their faces and front hair were painted. The rest of the party were dressed like good, stock-raising American farmers, but were unmistakably Indians. I was told there was a father with six sons in the party, all very large, broad-shouldered men. They filed quietly into their seats, preceded by a local guide, in whose hands they seemed like good, docile children.

They had come to town to get their government allowance, and our local agent induced them to take in the show. It was doubtless a case of reciprocity, for we certainly "took them in." One can never know what they thought of us, but one can do something in the way of inference. They sat quite immovable in their seats, with their ox-like eyes fixed on our party while we played serious music. No shadow of emotion could be seen on their countenances.

The fifth number of the programme was a violin solo played by Mr. Schultze, and for an encore he gave a little *caprice* entitled, *The Bird in the Tree*, a charming *jeu d'esprit*, by Miska Hauser, which represents the joyful, almost delirious, singing of a wild bird in the woods. The moment Mr. Schultze began this piece, the Indians were all alive, their eyes sparkled with pleasure, and they nudged each other with their elbows. And when the little

OTTO HEGNER AND HIS FATHER. *Page* 246

bird-melody and imitations of bird singing began (all done in high harmonic, flageolet tones on the violin), they looked all around the ceiling and the walls, doubtless expecting to see singing-birds flitting about. Not seeing any, they looked at the violinist, and began to understand that he was the magician. The surprise, and almost incredulity, which was depicted on the faces of these children of nature was a rare show in itself. At its conclusion they jumped up and down just as little children do when something unusual pleases them.

This violin piece ended the first part of the programme. Our second part began with another serious piece, and the twelve pairs of eyes lapsed into the ox-like placidity again. Very shortly the red men had had enough of us "freaks," and they quietly rose and filed out of the hall.

In this same Topeka, many years later, the concluding piece on one of our programmes was a *potpourri* which began with the introduction to the *Der Freischütz* overture. We had a good house and a crowded gallery. In the latter two men were seated on the right-hand side near the stage, who, when we began the closing piece, attempted to get out. They had to walk down one side of the hall, then across the end, then up the other side, before reaching the door, which was the only means of ingress or egress to the gallery—an awful fire-trap. We began the introduction to the overture. At this point, up rose the two men and started for the door. We stopped playing. The silence told the men that something had happened, and they sat down again, probably not wishing to make a show of themselves by walking out, in their number elevens, without music. All being quiet, we began the opening phrase once more; up rose again the two men and began their march. Again we stopped, wishing to let them get out and not have our piece spoiled; and again they stood still, this time in the aisle next the wall. We waited a little, and hearing no noise we began for the third time. Instantly, one of the men, who at this point had probably "got his mad up," started for the door. With him it was "Pike's Peak or bust" this time. When we heard the noise we stopped again, whereupon the audience began to titter, and the man making for the door ran the gauntlet of many ironical remarks from the boys, such as, "Take your time, old fellow,"—"No hurry,"—"He'll get there,"—"The fiddles'll wait," etc. Finally he reached the door and slammed it with all his might, a parting benediction which, as a reverend friend afterward remarked, said "Damn!" as surely as a word could be translated into action. The entire audience understood it in that sense and burst into a perfect roar of laughter.

When quiet was restored we played the piece, and ended the concert.

Many of our young and inexperienced friends probably think we have led a very sunny life, flitting from one scene of enjoyment to another. Perhaps we have had our share of good times; but I know to a certainty that we have had to take our share of hardships while travelling in the West thirty years ago. Railroads were not so plentiful as now, and we often had to travel on boats and in stage-coaches.

We had given a concert in Winona, Minn., and were booked next evening for La Crosse, Wis., twenty-six miles distant, both places being on the Mississippi River. It was planned that we should take a boat at six A.M. We were called and had breakfast in good season, but the boat did not show up. About ten A.M., word came that she had encountered a severe storm up-river, and would not reach Winona till about ten in the evening. There was a regular mail-boat which left Winona at four o'clock in the afternoon, in time to reach La Crosse at eight in the evening; but that was rather late to arrive, as the landing was a good mile distant from town. Desiring to fill our engagement in proper time and shape, I sought advice, and finally arranged with a livery-stable man to convey us by land. We did not get started until eleven in the forenoon; then we were packed, seven in number, into a canvas-covered wagon, a genuine "prairie schooner." We had eight heavy trunks, making a considerable load.

I had bargained to pay the man thirty-five dollars, and he agreed to land us in La Crosse by five or six o'clock in the evening. As soon as we were all loaded, he demanded his money in advance. Like an idiot (I did not know the world so well then as I did later) I paid it. We lost time in crossing the river, and it was after twelve o'clock before we reached the Wisconsin shore. We then had a drive of about eight miles of bottom-land through the woods,—a drive of the most jolting, dislocating, seasickening character, accompanied with the constant expectation of being capsized. In fact it was simply horrible. We were shut up suffocatingly close under the canvas, for it was midwinter and extremely cold.

About four in the afternoon we had climbed to a plateau above the bottom-lands, and drew up in front of a big barn with a little house attached to it, where we got out of our prairie schooner, hoping to get something in the line of food. A very hard-worked, careworn-looking woman told us she had nothing in the house but salt pork and potatoes; with tea, but no coffee, and neither bread nor crackers. We asked her to make some tea, which she did; but as the stablemen quickly changed horses and cried "All aboard!" we could swallow but little of the scalding-hot beverage.

As we started I casually asked our driver what time he expected to reach La Crosse, —and he thought we might get there between nine and ten! That reply made my heart sink. I expostulated, saying, "You know the liveryman agreed to deliver us at six P.M. at the latest." The driver replied, "It is impossible; we are still seventeen miles from La Crosse."

I then understood our dilemma, and the blunder we had made by not taking the mail-steamer, and also by paying in advance. We were in the clutches of unprincipled men.

After considering for a while what I could do to better the situation, I untied the canvas where I sat, told the driver to put his head near to me, and whispered into his ear, "If you can get us into La Crosse by eight P.M., you personally will be ten dollars richer." He replied, "All right; I'll do it."

From that time he labored hard for it, and almost overturned us when descending a steep hill leading to the Blackwater River, a narrow and shallow stream which we had to cross on a flat-bottomed ferry-boat, run on a wire. When about half-way over, we stuck on a sand-bank, and the order came, "Turn out all hands and help to pole her off." The ferrymen got into the shallow water on the bank and pried the boat off; we lost a good thirty minutes by that mishap, but it rested our horses, and we were rushed forward, and finally reached the opera house at 8.15. As we got out, we heard the mail-boat whistle!

Dead tired, hungry, without even a chance to wash our hands or brush our hair, and wearing clothes in which we had travelled, we unpacked our instruments and music, and went through the entire programme, doing our best to play and sing for the pleasure of the large audience. In the midst of our first piece we heard the rattle of carriages which had been sent to the boat to transfer us quickly to the opera house. The drivers brought up word, "Not aboard," and then learned we had come overland and were performing on the stage. When starting from Winona we could not telegraph, as the wires were down.

That was a day not easily forgotten,—no food from five o'clock in the morning till eleven at night, and bitter cold weather. But people can do wonders when duty forces them on.

I recall another very disagreeable journey for which some fortitude was necessary. We had played at a concert in Honesdale, Pennsylvania, and were booked for Montrose the following night. We had arranged to take a "gravity road" to Scranton, twenty-four miles distant, but a heavy snow-storm had blocked it up; no train could run; and the question arose, could we not be carried by sleighs? Duty was spurring us on to meet our engagement and earn our fees. We went to a liveryman, who said he would get us to Scranton in time for the afternoon train to Montrose Junction, or he would make no charge for the effort. That was a good principle to work on.

We agreed to start at six in the morning. The weather was clear but very cold. Our seven people and the driver were in a three-seated open sleigh, while the eight trunks and the double-bass (in a large, heavy case) were in a "pung." We took plenty of shovels with us, as our road was over a mountainous region. Many times we had to take down stone and wooden fences to get out of snow-drifts into open fields on clear ridges. The pung and baggage were, of course, the impedimenta; we had to unload and shovel out very often. About ten o'clock we came to a small village at the foot of a hill, where we got some coffee, and where the people declared that we could not possibly get over the next hill, as the road was full of drifts; but our driver was confident of success, and inspired us with his pluck. We started again, and encountered many difficulties. We upset twice while driving into fields; and once all our people were thrown into a ditch, the sleigh completely covering us, but our driver crawled out and helped us out. The atmosphere just then was heavy with mutterings, but Miss Ella Lewis, our brave and bright singer from Maine, kept our tempers sweet by infusing into us the hopefulness of her own steady courage. What a lucky thing it is for mankind in general to have a woman near when trouble comes!

We were making very slow progress, and began to despair of reaching Scranton; but about one o'clock we saw men and teams getting out ice in a valley below us, when we knew that our chances were favorable; and we really got there with half an hour to spare. We had a good dinner, gave our benedictions to the brave liveryman, and took the train for Montrose Junction. There was another steep mountain to climb, but I had telegraphed the Montrose people that we were coming, and they sent us special teams, for the snow-drifts were deep. We finally reached the hotel at half-past seven. The people gave us a right royal welcome, for they fully appreciated our heroic struggle to fill our engagement; and we were happy because our efforts had been crowned with success.

Printers have played some funny tricks with our programmes at times. It is a dangerous thing not to see a "proof" before printing, but often the programme has to be "rushed," and there is no opportunity. One of our violinists was to play a solo on the old French air, "*Je suis le petit tambour.*" When the concert was over, my attention was called to this number on the programme, which read, to my horror, "*Jesus le petit tambour.*"

At another time, Mr. Schultze was playing nightly the old *caprice* by Miska Hauser, entitled, *The Bird in the Tree*. Writing the programme one day in the office of the printer, I incautiously wrote, "Bird business, Mr. Schultze," supposing that they would print the full title as usual. The programmes were printed without giving me a chance to read the proof. When we came to that special number, we noticed a peculiar buzz and fun-enjoying condition among our auditors. When the concert was over, we inquired the cause, and a friend replied, handing us a programme, "We wanted to know when Mr. Schultze was to begin his 'bird business.'" It was a funny way to learn a useful lesson.

CHAPTER XXX

AMONG the many musicians with whom I have been brought into contact from time to time, there are some who, for reasons personal or musical, or both, seem to deserve special mention before I close these recollections.

One of them is J. C. D. Parker, a thorough American, born in Boston. His father was a steadfast member and worker of the Handel and Haydn Society. Mr. Parker, Jr., was from childhood a loving student of music, although for a time after his graduation at Harvard in 1848, he studied law; but eventually his strong musical bent rebelled against the giving up of his life to a profession for which he had no hearty inclination. At that period the Mendelssohn Quintette Club was doing a deal of hard studying, and young Parker was a constant and welcome visitor at our rehearsals. It is probable that our club is responsible for whatever trouble or loss may have come to him through having made music his life-work. At all events he finally started for Leipsic, and devoted himself to study for three or four years under skilful teachers.

Returning to Boston in 1854, he became one of our fine concert pianists, playing concertos in the Harvard Society concerts and most of the chamber works in those of the Mendelssohn Quintette Club. His solid reputation, however, has been earned as a composer. He is also well known by his fine translations of foreign works on harmony, which have been of the greatest service to musicians.

Although born in Germany, Ernst Perabo was brought to this country as a child in 1852, and can be considered a good American by this time. He received most of his fine musical training in the Leipsic Conservatory, but returned to this country in 1865, and continued his piano studies here. While still a young man he ventured on a public performance in New York City, where the critics promptly discovered that he was a consummately fine pianist. Shortly after, he came to Boston and made a successful *début* in one of the Harvard Society concerts, playing with great *éclat* the Hummel Septette.

Since then he has been one of our most progressive artists, and stands by right in the front rank. Though he has played most of the great modern compositions, his specialty is his fine rendering of Beethoven's works. As a teacher he is held in high esteem. Altogether, he is an earnest, thinking musician, who brings to our little musical world new and bright ideas.

He has made a lengthy list of the most useful arrangements for the pianoforte from various orchestral and other works.

Arthur Foote, born in Salem, Mass., is an American musician of enviable reputation,— a first-class pianist and organist, and a composer of high degree. His musical training has all been obtained in this country; from Stephen Emery in harmony, B. J. Lang in piano and organ, and J. K. Paine in composition. But after all, and best of all, he has dug the most valuable part of his acquirements out of himself,—*aus eigener Kraft*, as the Germans would say.

As a composer he has presented us with a long list of fine works, including most charming songs; while his larger compositions have been played and sung in the best concerts throughout the country. And as he is still in the prime of life it is to be hoped that he will produce many more works from that fine musical vein which he so abundantly possesses,— a vein of warm, rare musical feeling, aptly controlled by musical science.

Portland, Maine, has the honor of being the birthplace of J. K. Paine, who is easily one of the foremost American composers of music in classic form. His works include organ, chamber, symphonic, and oratorio music; and he is a practical organist of marked ability. Most of his training was received in Germany; and while he was there he composed a mass for grand orchestra, solos, and chorus, which was produced under his direction in Berlin, and to which the press of that city gave unstinted praise. Since his return to America in 1861, he has proved himself to be a most industrious and capable artist.

So much public praise has been given to him and his works that there is no need for me to add to it; it gives me pleasure, nevertheless, to express my sincere admiration of his genius. Harvard University honored itself and the art of music when it appointed Mr. Paine to a professorship in its faculty. It was a good example which has been followed by other seats of learning.

In approaching the name of my dear son-in-law, George William Sumner, so much of sor-

GEORGE W. SUMNER.

row at his untimely death fills my heart that I am unfitted to say what his memory deserves.

My acquaintance with Mr. Sumner began when I was searching for good pianoforte teachers for the National College of Music. Inquiries made among the older artists usually brought out strong recommendations of "young Sumner." He therefore became one of our teachers, and it was not long before he married my oldest daughter. He was a fine fellow, and when he was taken from us he left a void impossible to fill.

The testimony of history, when it refers to the life of a good man, remains a precious legacy to all who loved the subject. I therefore quote from the Boston *Transcript* of August, 1890:

"Mr. George W. Sumner was born of a musical family in Spencer, Mass., in 1848. He early showed his musical proclivities, and while still a child displayed enough talent to warrant his exhibition in public. His father, however,—Mr. William Sumner, for many years a teacher and music dealer in Worcester,—took pains to have the boy's education properly directed, and to that end placed him under the best available instructors, Mr. B. J. Lang being the last one.

"Mr. Sumner's proficiency as a pianist, organist, and teacher was of high character. His appearances as a performer of pianoforte concertos in the 'Harvard' and the 'Boston Symphony' Societies, as a pianist in chamber concerts, or as accompanist at the piano or organ with the 'Handel and Haydn Society,' the 'Cecilia,' the 'Apollo,' and 'Boylston' Clubs, were alike creditable to the occasion, to his art, and to himself.

"Mr. Sumner's longest term of service as a church organist was in the Arlington Street Church, where for eighteen years he had charge of the music, and displayed no little talent in composition; but these compositions were all in the line of hymns or anthems, and few were ever published. Two notable pieces are in use in all churches, *When Winds are Raging* and *Let your Light so Shine*. This latter is an alto solo.

"In 1879, Mr. Sumner was appointed director of the Orpheus Club, of Springfield, Mass. He brought the Club to a high rank among male-voice choirs. His musical tastes, though refined and exacting, were broad and comprehensive. Personally, he was a man of genial temperament, unaffected and sincere.

"He left a widow, the daughter of Mr. Thomas Ryan, and a young daughter."

Mr. John S. Dwight also contributed a notice in the Boston *Transcript*, which testifies to the respect Mr. Sumner had inspired among his professional brethren:

"In Memoriam: George William Sumner.— The musical tribute paid to the memory of this gifted, serviceable, generous, and amiable young artist by his professional associates and hosts of friends, at the Music Hall on Tuesday afternoon, November 25th, was a touching and memorable occasion. The great Hall was

Recollections of an Old Musician

at least two thirds filled with sympathetic, serious listeners. Nearly all the leading singers, pianists, teachers, composers, and high-class musicians of our city, lent their aid most heartily to the carrying out of a significant and worthy programme. The list of participants included all these names:

"Mr. Carl Baermann, Mr. George Chadwick, Miss Gertrude Edmands, Mr. Carl Faelten, Mrs. E. C. Fenderson, Mr. Arthur Foote, Miss Gertrude Franklin, Miss Elizabeth Hamlin, Mr. Clarence E. Hay, Mr. Anton Hekking ('cellist), Mr. Franz Kneisel (concert-master), Mr. Gardner S. Lamson, Mr. B. J. Lang, Mr. E. A. MacDowell, Mrs. Gertrude Swayne Matthews, Mr. Ivan Morawski, Mr. Ethelbert Nevin, Mr. Arthur Nikisch (symphony conductor), Mr. George J. Parker, Mr. Ernst Perabo, Mr. Carl Pfluger, Mr. Joshua Phippen, Miss Louise Rollwagen, Mr. J. H. Ricketson, Mr. Sullivan A. Sargent, Mrs. J. E. Tippett, Mr. H. G. Tucker, Mrs. Jennie Patrick Walker, Mr. B. L. Whelpley, Miss Harriet Whiting, Mr. Arthur Whiting, Mr. William J. Winch, Mr. Carl Zerrahn (oratorio director)."

Of this concert the Boston *Herald* said:

"The most remarkable programme arranged in recent years was prepared for the concert in memory of George William Sumner, whose recent death deprived the Arlington Street Church of its accomplished musical director, and left a vacancy in a wide circle of friends that will not soon be forgotten."

CHAPTER XXXI

WHILE the Civil War was going on, the government was already planning soldiers' homes for the battered and crippled men left in its terrible wake. The first Home was more like a hospital for invalids than it was strictly a Home, and was established in the suburbs of Milwaukee.

The Quintette Club being in that city, I happened to meet Ex-Governor Smith of New Hampshire, with whom I had a slight acquaintance; and who told me that he and the other commissioners appointed by the government to build and look after these Homes, had arranged to visit the new buildings on the following morning, go through with the formality of acceptance, and have the first flag-raising. He invited me to bring our club, and contribute a little music for the occasion, which we gladly agreed to do.

Next morning about six to eight carriage loads of citizens, with the commissioners and our party, started for the Home, where the

THE MENDELSSOHN QUINTETTE CLUB.

ceremony was to take place at precisely twelve o'clock. It was a very unpropitious morning; a furious gale was "blowing great guns," and it was difficult to face it and stand upright. The little company of war-scarred veterans in the Home, perhaps a hundred in number, were drawn up in line to receive us,—many of them with only one leg or one arm, or on crutches, truly a saddening sight.

The formal acceptance of the building by the commissioners took place in the house; then the invited guests assembled near the flagstaff. Music was out of the question; our nice little plans for that were sadly frustrated by Æolus the god of winds. I determined, nevertheless, not to let that flag go up without some music. I took my clarinet to the foot of the flagstaff, and when " Old Glory " was hauled up I played as lustily as I could the *Star Spangled Banner*. At the conclusion, all present gave three cheers. It was a short ceremony, and we were glad to get under shelter once more.

Six or eight years ago, our club gave a concert in the Home, which is now a truly wonderful institution, one of which any nation may justly be proud. Indeed the present Home is quite a little city in itself; with a charming opera house, which will hold about one thousand persons and has its own regular orchestra. The Home is often visited by musical and dramatic companies. Everything of a nature to cheer up the old veterans is freely encouraged.

While performing on the evening in question, my mind was busy. I could not forget that I was the son of an old soldier, my father having served for thirty-three years. One of my brothers also served under the British flag and lies buried in India. My youngest brother served all through the Civil War in the Union army, and had a good record as Captain in the 1st N. Y. Mounted Rifles. He did not long survive his campaigning.

When I looked over the rows of white-headed men, I thought of the peculiar bond of sympathy which must exist among them. Many were seated alongside of the very comrades who had stood shoulder to shoulder with them in the hour of supreme danger, when each minute might bring the billet for eternal separation. Amid the tumult of action, when smoke and flame, shot and shell, make earth to disappear and a hell to take its place, the elbow touch alone gives the signal, " Still alive." In such moments a fellowship is formed which has no counterpart among men's associations.

I took occasion between the parts of the concert to address the audience and recall the part we had played, over thirty years before, at the dedication and flag-raising: and I noticed that my remarks raised quite a buzz in various parts of the hall. Afterwards I learned that there was a number of men still in the Home who corroborated my story. Indeed the episode was one not easily forgotten. The furious gale, the crippled men clinging to and supporting each other when they took off their hats to cheer the upgoing flag, for which they had fought, made a scene worthy the pencil of an artist.

Many years ago we gave a first concert in a certain small town in Iowa. In the front seats of the concert room sat a good, hearty-looking German with his "frau" and children, all of whom had elated, interested faces. Evidently national pride was stirred in their hearts by the names of the performers; and it found vent and expression at the end of the first piece, when the German rose to his feet and shouted out, "Bully for the Dutch!"

Afterwards we were informed that this good honest German had been buzzing round town, days in advance of the concert, telling his

American friends, "Now you will something hear like music." After the concert we were right royally entertained by our enthusiastic friend, who claimed that all musicians were good Germans.

CHAPTER XXXII

THANKFULLY I reach the last chapter of "An Old Musician's Recollections"—and will end them by relating a pleasant experience I had, some eight or ten years ago, on my first visit to Berlin.

Desiring to pay my respects to the great master-violinist, Joachim, I called at his house and sent up my card. I was at once received and Mr. Joachim gave me a cordial greeting, and put me at ease by saying, "You are one of us. I know all that you and your club have been doing ; I welcome you to Berlin." The speech was uttered in good square American, and in a warm, genial tone of voice.

Having made as long a call as I dared to make on a busy man, I rose to leave, saying : "Mr. Joachim, I have never had the pleasure of hearing you play, and I very much fear that I never shall, for I understand that you don't like ocean travel. My only chance to hear you may be at the present moment."

" I would play with great pleasure" he replied, "but I have an appointment at the High School for Music; perhaps you would like to go over there with me"; adding, "Would you not like to hear our quartette play?"

My delight at the possibility of such a pleasure must have shown itself in my face, as he promptly arranged a meeting for the next morning; and it was a most enjoyable, musical, and social *matinée bei Joachim*. The four gentlemen of his quartette certainly did me great honor when they devoted a morning to my pleasure, simply because I was a brother artist from America. They played the F-minor No. 10 Quartette by Beethoven, and a new quartette in manuscript by D'Albert. Joachim played violin *primo;* D'Ahna, *secundo;* Wirt, viola; Hausemann, violoncello.

All four of them were professors in the High School, Joachim being the general director and chief of the institution. The school is mainly supported by the government, and it is chiefly for orchestral instruments, though piano and singing are taught. It is almost exclusively attended by those who are preparing for professional life. Pupils are rigorously examined, and none can enter without good qualifications.

I heard the pupils play symphonies and difficult concert overtures,—also cantatas with solo singing and chorus. Perhaps one fourth of the "string" performers were young ladies, and several were Americans whom I knew; Miss Geraldine Morgan, now in New York, was at the first desk of violins, and Miss Lucy Campbell played the violoncello. There was also a number of young men from America. Among them was a modest young man from Louisville, just entered. He told me he had been incited to study the violin by hearing our Quintette Club, and hoped it would be his good fortune some day to play with us. Some seasons ago, I needed a first violin for the Club, and the modest boy, who had developed into a brilliant player, became for a season my concert-master,—Mr. Sol Marcosson.

Now, after fifty-four years of service,—forty-nine of them with the Quintette Club,—rarely free from care and responsibility,—I think I can honestly say that I have tried to do my share of musical duty. There have been numberless times when much fortitude was needed to continue working, for seasons were bad and incomes small. But there was a good spirit which said to me, "Continue to do the work for which you are best fitted, and your reward will come later."

I have often felt a great satisfaction welling up within me—a something which caused me to feel perfectly happy—when the playing of the Club was quite "up to the mark"; that was for me a wonderfully sustaining power.

I began life in America when the art of music was about in accordance with my age,—that of a youth. The art has grown, will continue to grow, and will become more and more of a delight to all our people. There will be no decadence.

To the old friends who have followed me in this retrospection, I venture to express the hope that I may have a place in their good memory to the end of their days. For my unknown readers,—perhaps a very small contingent,—I trust that they will find something of interest or value to repay them for the time given to "An Old Musician's Recollections."

THOMAS RYAN.

FINIS

www.ingramcontent.com/pod-product-compliance
Lightning Source LLC
Chambersburg PA
CBHW030357230426
43664CB00007BB/634